WALKING IN PORTUGAL

Acknowledgements

We would like to thank our publisher for giving two untried and inexperienced writers this exciting opportunity. Also to the staff at various Institute for Nature Conservation and Forests (ICNF) offices and tourist information bureaux for their assistance, to the complete strangers encountered on these walks for offers of sustenance, and most importantly to the people of Portugal for being so welcoming.

Additional thanks to our friends and family for help and forbearance.

WALKING IN PORTUGAL

40 GRADED SHORT AND MULTI-DAY WALKS INCLUDING SERRA DA ESTRELA AND PENEDA GERÊS NATIONAL PARK

by Andrew Mok and Simon Whitmarsh

JUNIPER HOUSE, MURLEY MOSS,
OXENHOLME ROAD, KENDAL, CUMBRIA LA9 7RL
www.cicerone.co.uk

© Andrew Mok and Simon Whitmarsh 2018
First edition 2018
ISBN: 978 1 85284 889 7
Reprinted 2022, 2024 (with updates)

Printed in China on responsibly sourced paper on behalf of Latitude Press Ltd.
A catalogue record for this book is available from the British Library.
All photographs are by the author unless otherwise stated.

Route mapping by Lovell Johns www.lovelljohns.com
Contains OpenStreetMap.org data © OpenStreetMap
contributors, CC-BY-SA. NASA relief data courtesy of ESRI

Updates to this guide

While every effort is made by our authors to ensure the accuracy of guidebooks as they go to print, changes can occur during the lifetime of an edition. Any updates that we know of for this guide will be on the Cicerone website (www. cicerone.co.uk/889/updates), so please check before planning your trip. We also advise that you check information about such things as transport, accommodation and shops locally. Even rights of way can be altered over time.

The route maps in this guide are derived from publicly available data, databases and crowd-sourced data. As such they have not been through the detailed checking procedures that would generally be applied to a published map from an official mapping agency, although naturally we have reviewed them closely in the light of local knowledge as part of the preparation of this guide.

We are always grateful for information about any discrepancies between a guidebook and the facts on the ground, sent by email to updates@cicerone. co.uk.

Register your book: To sign up to receive free updates, special offers and GPX files, create a Cicerone account and register your purchase via the 'My Account' tab at www.cicerone.co.uk.

Front cover: Walking towards the summit of Poios Brancos with views of the pitchers surrounding Torre, the highest point in mainland Portugal (Walk 24)

CONTENTS

Mountain safety

Every mountain walk has its dangers, and those described in this guidebook are no exception. All who walk or climb in the mountains should recognise this and take responsibility for themselves and their companions along the way. The author and publisher have made every effort to ensure that the information contained in this guide was correct when it went to press, but, except for any liability that cannot be excluded by law, they cannot accept responsibility for any loss, injury or inconvenience sustained by any person using this book.

International Distress Signal *(emergency only)*
Six blasts on a whistle (and flashes with a torch after dark) spaced evenly for one minute, followed by a minute's pause. Repeat until an answer is received. The response is three signals per minute followed by a minute's pause.

Helicopter Rescue
The following signals are used to communicate with a helicopter:

Help needed:
raise both arms
above head to
form a 'Y'

Help not needed:
raise one arm
above head, extend
other arm downward

Emergency telephone numbers
Emergency Services: tel 112
Forest Fires: tel 117

Note There is no mountain rescue service in Portugal. Health care can be expensive – be adequately insured.

Standing at the Fisgas de Ermelo official viewpoint, Alvão

Symbols used on route maps

route

alternative route

long-distance trail

start

finsh

start/finish point

alternative start point

alternative start/finish point

woodland

urban areas

international border

station/railway

peak

shelter

building

chapel/monastery/cross

castle/fort

bridge

viewpoint (*miradouro*)

windmill or turbine/tall cairn/
radio or aerial mast/lighthouse

picnic area/beach

waterfalls (*cascata*)

water feature

other feature

Relief
in metres

2200–2400

2000–2200

1800–2000

1600–1800

1400–1600

1200–1400

1000–1200

800–1000

600–800

400–600

200–400

0–200

SCALE: 1:50,000

0 kilometres 0.5   1

0 miles   0.5

Contour lines are
drawn at 25m intervals
and highlighted at
100m intervals.

GPX files

GPX files for all routes can
be downloaded for free at
www.cicerone.co.uk/889/GPX

A typical inland landscape of southern Portugal with rock roses, lavender, and a profusion of wildflowers

PREFACE

Our first experience of walking in Portugal came during a year of European travelling, when we were captivated by the unexpectedly huge mountains, devoid of crowds, and numerous excellent walking trails. Finding out where these began or went proved to be challenging, with limited resources from the majority of tourist information offices, poor outdated maps and no guidebook in English. The solution was to do extensive research and write our own guide.

We do not pretend to have walked every single footpath in Portugal but have investigated hundreds: asking locals, going online, making enquiries at the national park, nature park and tourist information offices, poring over maps, or simply spotting the signs as we went along. From these hundreds we have walked more than a hundred, from which we have selected walks that made our hearts sing, our spirits lift and made us feel glad to be alive. This is of course entirely subjective. Wherever possible we have chosen walks along the 'old ways' (routes used by villagers in ancient times as their sole means of passage), sections of long-distance GR trails, and incorporating some history.

This book is designed to complement the Cicerone guide *Walking in the Algarve*, and has a different selection of Algarvian routes.

Simon Whitmarsh and Andrew Mok
2017

View of the town from Marvão's castle, São Mamede (Walk 31)

INTRODUCTION

The Azeite – 'Olive oil' – route follows cobbled paths next to olive groves (Walk 15)

Why go walking in Portugal? This delightful country enchanted two self-confessed walking addicts so much that after just a short visit we were captivated, returning again and again. There are so many reasons to fall in love with this relatively undiscovered gem of a country. The diverse terrain includes the rugged north with a multitude of mountains, many higher than Ben Nevis, and the beautiful Douro valley. Further south, the Serra da Estrela mountain range provides alpine, snow-capped peaks and plateaux. There is nearly 1000km of coastline including the dramatic arid scenery of the southern coastal areas, bordered by wave-pummelled cliffs.

All this is encapsulated in a narrow strip of the Iberian Peninsula.

Another reason is the weather. With such a variety of meteorological microclimates within its borders, there is always somewhere to enjoy hiking at any time of the year in Portugal. The Arrábida Nature Park is good for walking in winter, as is the Algarve, whereas in the heights of summer when it is too hot to enjoy a good walk in many parts of Europe, you will find balmy temperatures in Serra da Estrela Nature Park.

The major draw remains the space. This is not a large country compared to its more massive Iberian neighbour, but you will be able to walk in peace and tranquillity, very likely in the delights of just your own company. Even if its popularity as a walking destination were to increase over time, this is a place that could absorb many visitors. In addition, there are the warm and friendly people. For those who don't speak Portuguese, some effort plus sign-language will be rewarded with smiles and helpfulness.

And then there are the wildlife and flowers. The hillsides carpeted with fragrant blooms in spring, or the almond blossom of late winter lying like snow on the ground are truly a sight to behold. Should you wish to be surrounded by trees, Portugal is the world's largest cork producer and has widespread arboriculture. The birdwatching is phenomenal with a plethora of resident raptors, and uncountable millions of migratory birds. You may even be lucky enough to spot an Iberian wolf in Peneda-Gerês National Park, or a previously extinct lynx in Guadiana Nature Reserve.

These selected walks take you on a 175 million-year journey through time. From fossilised dinosaur footprints in Arrábida (Walk 28), via megalithic sites around Monsaraz (Walk 33), and the Roman roads from Portugal all the way to Spain (Walk 9), to the deserted schist villages that are now undergoing a resurgence, becoming superb bases for outdoor activities (Walk 17). Allow some time on your visit to see why UNESCO has

decided that Portugal deserves to be the proud home of a dozen World Heritage Sites.

The food and drink is another understated attraction, with the unsung hero being the desserts and the *doces conventuais* (convent sweets). The good, heavy rich red wines from the Douro or Tejo valleys could compete with those of Bordeaux, but as their best are not often exported, you will have to come here to sample them. The same applies to the crisp *vinho verde* from Minho.

This is just a taste of our experiences after walking more than 6000km over a period of three years. Enjoy these favourite routes in Portugal. *Boa viagem!*

ABOUT PORTUGAL

To many people, the country's best-known region may be the Algarve, but there's a whole lot more to Portugal – especially for the walker. There are mountains upon mountains, and huge amounts of space, nature and solitude. Portugal has a population density only a quarter of England's, so even though it is a smaller country there is much more space.

Adding further to the under-crowding is that most Portuguese do not walk for leisure. One local explained that 'during the dictatorship, we all had to walk. Now that we don't, why should we?' Often when the Portuguese do walk they do so in big groups of up to 400 at a time, as

Panoramic view of Manteigas and the Zêzere glacial valley (Walk 23) with Penhas Douradas above (Walk 21)

a pilgrimage, a short walk with a long lunch, or a torch-lit night walk.

This is a relatively undeveloped country in some ways – where else in Europe would you expect to find people washing clothes by hand in communal *lavadouros* – yet surprisingly ahead of its time in others. It is astonishingly green in terms of energy production and usage, with 63% of all energy used in 2014 being from renewable sources: mainly wind turbines (as seen on Walk 26) and hydro-electric (Walk 17).

In Portugal, high places are often punctuated with radio aerial masts and accessible by road, so don't expect pristine summits apart from on top of Carris (Walk 7) and the Montesinho peaks (Walk 12). Other summits are graced with beautiful chapels, such as São João da Fraga

(Walk 6), Monte Farinha (Walk 13) and Peninha (Walk 27), or with castles such as Castro Laboreiro (Walk 2) and Marvão (Walk 31).

Freshwater swimming is another particular delight in Portugal; a *praia fluvial* is a freshwater beach, either on a riverbank or on the shores of a reservoir. There are opportunities on Walks 7, 8, 9, 17 and 29.

GEOLOGY

The geology of Portugal cannot be covered in full here, but to put it in a nutshell, Portugal has three main geological areas: north, central and southern. The north is essentially a stack of five layers raised when the Iberian plate collided with the Meguma Terrane plate 410 million years ago. This collision formed the mountains of the Picos de Europa, Montesinho and Peneda-Gerês. Its top layer is sedimentary schist (pronounced 'shist'), a metamorphic rock formed when mudstone has been highly compressed and heated. The word comes from the Greek *skhistos*, meaning to split (see Walks 17 to 19). Revealed by the erosive forces of the Rio Douro is Miranda do Douro gneiss, the lowest layer of the stack and the oldest rocks in Portugal, which are pre-Cambrian (about 600 million years old). Another stripe in this stack is granite, evident in Peneda-Gerês (also with much evidence of glaciation, such as moraines and erratic blocks), Montesinho and Alvão.

The central portion of Portugal is mostly sedimentary rocks from the Cenozoic and Mesozoic basins – notably the massive Jurassic limestone deposits in Aire e Candeeiros Nature Park. This porous rock contains at least 1500 caves, including the biggest and most stalagmite-decorated, Mira de Aire, and the best dinosaur footprints (at Monumento Natural das Pegadas dos Dinossáurios da Serra de Aire). Along the coast, the limestone is mixed with other rocks, both sedimentary and igneous, left over from the formation of the North Atlantic. The coastline is very rocky, indented by small bays with white sandy beaches and usually surmounted by cliffs of considerable height. Dinosaur footprints are also found here (Walk 28). Serra da Estrela features the most dramatic evidence of Portugal's

ice-age existence with the gigantic glaciated Zêzere valley (Walk 23).

The southern geological area is from a separate continent and the rocks are much younger – from the Upper Devonian to Carboniferous eras – and are mostly sedimentary. They form stunning cliffs along the coastline, as witnessed on Walks 34 and 35.

HISTORY

What we now call Portugal has been inhabited since prehistory, as evidenced by the astounding 27,000-year-old rock carvings found near Vila Nova de Foz Côa (near Walks 15 and 16). It was then colonised by the Phoenicians, followed by the Celts. The Romans took about 200 years to conquer the area, facing great resistance from the feisty northern tribes. The best Roman archaeological sites are to be found in Conímbriga, near Coimbra.

After the fall of the Roman Empire, the Suevi occupied the north of the Iberian Peninsula, and the Visigoths (who introduced Christianity to the region) the south. They were both replaced by the Moors, who were evicted in the *Reconquista* (reconquest) ending in 1249, fully 250 years before Spain's *Reconquista*. During this, the country was officially separated from the rest of Iberia and the Kingdom of Portugal was founded in 1128, after the battle of São Mamede (see Walk 31). Alfonso Henrique, son of the victorious Count Henry, became the first Portuguese king.

Portugal has been linked with Britain by the oldest surviving international pact (the Treaty of Windsor, 1386). At one time Portugal was one of the richest and most powerful nations in the world, due to their navigational prowess exemplified by Prince Henry the navigator (whose trainees set sail from Capela do Senhor Jesus dos Navegantes, Walk 28), ruling an empire spanning five continents. The Treaty of Tordesillas (1494) dictated that of all the lands yet to be discovered, half should belong to the Portuguese.

The country was at war intermittently with Spain for hundreds of years, from the foundation of Portugal all the way until the French invasion of 1807, which was supported by Spain – leading to a rivalry comparable to that between the English and the French. This is likely to be why they have gone to such great lengths to ensure that despite both languages being derived from the same Latin roots dating from the Roman occupation, they sound so different. Portugal was involuntarily brought back under Spanish rule by Philip II of Spain (who then became Philip I of Portugal) in 1580 during the succession crisis – which later undermined the Treaty of Windsor, as the Spanish Armada contained some Portuguese ships.

The Portuguese War of Restoration, officially only ending in 1668, did not reverse the decline from the country's pre-eminence, further exacerbated by the Lisbon earthquake of 1755, and by Napoleon's invasion of 1807.

The First Republic violently removed the monarchy in 1910,

Chafurdãos – circular structures whose purpose remains unknown – can be seen in the São Mamede and Tejo area (Walk 29)

followed by severe political instability ending with a *coup d'etat* in 1926, which led into the Salazar dictatorship. Times were hard, and there were mass emigrations, with millions of people seeking a better life: those from the north went to Europe (hence the frequency with which French is spoken), and from the rest of the country mainly to Portuguese-speaking Brazil. Some villages were abandoned entirely, as can be seen on many walks, and in most places you will still see derelict buildings whose owners left in the diaspora.

The repression finally ended in the bloodless Carnation Revolution of 1974, following which Portugal joined the EEC in 1986, with mixed fortunes: they required an EU bailout in 2011.

WILDLIFE

Nature forms an important part of any outdoor activity, and the opportunities to see and enjoy it in Portugal exceed those throughout most of Europe. The Iberian grey wolf roams Peneda-Gerês. You are unlikely to see one, but may see the gnawed bones of their prey or their tracks, which look like huge dog prints of about 9–15cm diameter. There has never been a recorded wolf attack on humans in Portugal. Limited to the same area are roe deer, the symbol of the park, as are Spanish ibex. Red deer are more likely to be encountered in Guadiana, although the majority of their territory is within Spain.

Wild boar can be found in many rural areas and you are bound to see evidence of their foraging; Walk 22 is

White stork on a convent roof; they migrate to Africa in September, returning in February (Walk 33)

even named after them. Bears were extinct but are apparently beginning to make a return into Peneda-Gerês from northern Spain. The previously extinct Iberian lynx has been successfully reintroduced into Guadiana Nature Park. Two unexpected creatures are Egyptian mongoose and the genet, both introduced by the Moors to keep vermin under control.

Portugal is an undiscovered gem for anyone with an interest in birds, many species of which can be easily seen on walks. Egyptian vultures, griffon vultures, black vultures and golden eagles (called royal eagles here) abound in Tejo and Douro. There are many migratory birds such as the strikingly coloured bee-eaters and white storks. The latter are present all over Portugal, from spring to autumn; even when they have returned to Africa, their huge nests are a constant reminder of these sociable visitors.

Lizards are commonly encountered. There are about 20 different species, of which the most stunning is the Iberian Emerald Lizard (Schreiber's lizard). The 11 species of snakes are all rather shy, and only two are poisonous: Lataste's viper (with zigzag patterns on its back), found throughout Portugal, and the Portuguese viper (highly polymorphic with variable patterns or none, hence it is difficult to identify) in the far north. The endangered Mediterranean turtle may be seen by rivers and lakes in the south and the Iberian green frog is widespread throughout Portugal.

PLANTS AND FLOWERS

Portugal's national tree is the cork oak (*Quercus sobreiro*; see 'Agriculture', below), often found alongside Portuguese, holm, English and Pyrenean oaks. Also widespread is the strawberry tree (*Arbutus unedo*), unusual for its contemporaneous flowers and fruits, which are used to make the local alcoholic drink *Medronho*.

In spring there is an abundance of wildflowers: poppies, lavender, saxifrage, geraniums, buttercups, orchids, iris, broom, native rock rose, lupins and many more. In Estrela, spring begins around May whereas in the nearby but lower Douro it tends to start in March – and yet the almonds blossom a month earlier. Further south in the Algarve, the warmer temperature advances the flourish of spring flowers even further, meaning spring could be experienced from February until June in various parts of Portugal. As the temperature warms up, the unmissable aroma of herbs including sage, thyme, rosemary and mint can be experienced on the walks. To cope with the very hot and dry conditions in the summer, some plants have needle-like or furry leaves to reduce evaporation; cacti and succulents have thick waxy leaves to store water, while other plants become dormant

Miniature daffodils, Serra de Estrela; gum rockrose, which originated in Portugal; common rhododendron (endangered endemic Iberian subspecies), Monchique

and annuals set seed by early summer. In autumn, the golden grasses complement the colour of the clear blue skies.

The diverse growing conditions nurture a huge variety of plants. The dry and very mild winters in the Algarve, which has relatively sandy soil, attract temperate plants. On the Costa Vicentina, the very low-lying plants are able to withstand drying salt-laden Atlantic winds. Many are endemic to this region, including the local rock rose (*Cistus palhinhae*). In the north and more mountainous regions, plants have to be hardier to thrive in wet, cold conditions, being covered with snow for up to half the year.

AGRICULTURE

Arboriculture for wood, paper and cork is widespread in Portugal, which is the world's largest cork producer. The bark is stripped and dried without killing the tree, about every nine years. The tree is then labelled with a number; if marked '15' this means it was harvested in 2015 and will be ready again in 2024. The industry is in decline as wine producers are switching from natural to cheaper but less aesthetically pleasing options. However, screwtops' inability to breathe may cause sulphurisation and stop wine ageing properly, and their plastic lining degrades with time. In addition, while it is true that screwtops prevent cork taint, many would argue that the wine experience is poorer without the 'pop' of a cork.

The fast-growing acacia, eucalyptus and pine are all cultivated for paper pulp, but unfortunately they are more flammable. Australian acacia (*Acacia dealbata*) is very invasive and eucalyptus' deep taproots dry out the ground more than native trees. The result is an increased risk of forest fire, which is a major problem in Portugal. Also grown extensively are chestnuts (*Castanea*), mainly for animal feed, and stone pine (*Pinus pinea*) as an anti-erosion measure funded by the EU.

Smallholdings are common in rural areas, nowadays tended by aging populations. Unusual crops are grown, such as blue and yellow lupins for their edible seeds known as *tremoços*. A wide variety of grapes are grown throughout Portugal as delicious fruits or for wine. Douro, with its neat terraced vineyards along the river, is UNESCO-listed as the world's oldest denominated wine area. A distinctive Iberian, predominantly Portuguese structure is an *espigueiro* or *canastro* (granary), often still in use for the storing of maize, specially built to protect the contents from rodents.

Much land is used as pasture, with skinny sheep and goats widely seen across the country (the sheep cheeses are delicious), and some areas have their own breeds of cow (Peneda and Alvão). In Alentejo the pastures are dotted with holm oak, providing firewood for people and shade for livestock. Far fewer chemicals are used here, as evidenced by the prodigious amounts of wildflowers, resulting in excellent honey.

A pile of harvested cork drying in the sun

WEATHER

Portugal is a small country with a large range of weather conditions. The mainland can be climatically split into north and south. The mountains of the north create a barrier to Atlantic winds, trapping cool air and rain, the high rainfall encouraging greenery in abundance. Heading east and inland, summers become hotter and winters longer.

Inland and at altitude, snow is a regular occurrence, often settling for days. January sees highs of 6°C and lows down to -15°C while the peak of summer sees temperatures of around 28°C, although they can reach 40°C. The area has on average 123 rainy days per year and 20 days of snow. Serra da Estrela, the highest mountain range in Portugal, has a ski resort; snow is frequent and heavy here throughout winter.

Portugal's climate heats up and dries out heading south. Past Lisbon there is a typical Mediterranean climate consisting of mild winters, sunny warm springs, and scorching summers with temperatures frequently over 30°C. Further south it gets hotter and drier, with 300 days of sunshine in the Algarve.

Along the coastline the climate is predominantly influenced by the currents and winds of the Atlantic Ocean: summer highs are counteracted with a cooling sea breeze, while the ocean waters temper the winters.

For weather predictions, visit the Portuguese meteorological website (www.ipma.pt) or the independent www.meteoblue.com.

Part of the disused Fort of São Domingos da Baralha, built on the Chã dos Navagantes (Walk 28)

Temperatures (average low/high °C			
	Porto	**Lisbon**	**Faro**
Jan	5/14	8/15	7/16
Feb	6/15	9/16	8/17
Mar	7/17	10/18	9/19
Apr	9/18	12/19	11/20
May	11/19	13/21	13/22
Jun	14/23	16/25	16/26
Jul	16/25	18/28	18/29
Aug	15/25	18/28	19/29
Sep	14/24	17/26	17/27
Oct	12/20	15/22	14/23
Nov	8/17	12/18	11/20
Dec	7/14	10/15	9/17

Rainfall (mm/rainy days)			
	Porto	**Lisbon**	**Faro**
Jan	158/13	97/10	63/7
Feb	140/12	90/10	64/8
Mar	90/10	51/7	35/5
Apr	116/11	65/9	41/6
May	98/10	56/7	20/4
Jun	46/6	17/3	7/1
Jul	18/3	6/1	2/0
Aug	27/3	7/1	4/1
Sep	71/6	29/3	13/1
Oct	138/11	80/8	63/5
Nov	158/12	107/9	84/7
Dec	195/13	122/11	116/9

WHEN TO GO

There is always somewhere in Portugal to enjoy hiking at any time of the year. The temperature is most comfortable for walking in spring (March to May) and autumn (September and October). In general, the intense heat of the summer (July and August) could be a challenge. This is lessened by going along the coastline with the sea

23

breeze, or up the cooler mountains in the north; the mountains in Estrela could be covered with snow from October until May. However, these are popular summer destinations with the Portuguese and could be crowded. May to August is the period with less rainfall, and in general the south is much drier with Algarve claiming 300 days of sunshine per year on average (see 'Weather', above).

In order to admire the almond blossoms, January and February would be the best time to visit. Wildflowers in spring are truly a delight, and the autumnal colours are equally splendid; the timing varies across the different regions (see 'Plants and flowers', above). Migratory birds provide an extra reason to visit from March to October.

Every village and region has its own festival and pilgrimage that can provide unique experiences – but they can also cause significant traffic problems. The national celebrations like Fátima or Carnation Day are on a grand scale and are eye-openers.

Date	Portuguese name	English name	Comments
National public holidays			
1 January	Dia de Ano Novo	New Year's Day	
Variable	Carnival	Shrove Tuesday	The day before the first day of Lent
Variable	Sexta-Feira Santa	Good Friday	
Variable	Domingo de Páscoa	Easter Sunday	
25 April	Dia da Liberdade	Carnation Day	Celebrates the Carnation Revolution of 1974 (see 'History')
1 May	Dia do Trabalhador	Labour Day	
Variable	Corpus Christi	Corpus Christi	Thursday, 60 days after Easter Sunday
10 June	Dia de Portugal	Portuguese National Day	
15 August	Assunção de Nossa Senhora	Assumption	Ascension of Mary to Heaven
5 October	Implantação da República	Republic Day	Celebrates the end of the monarchy
1 November	Dia de todos os santos	All Saints' Day	
1 December	Restauração da Independência	Restoration of Independence	Celebrates Portugal becoming re-independent from Spain in 1668 (see 'History')

Date	Portuguese name	English name	Comments
8 December	Imaculada Conceição	Immaculate Conception	
25 December	Natal	Christmas Day	
26 December	Segunda Oitava	Boxing Day	
Regional festivals			
19 March	Dia de São José	St Joseph's Day	Santarém
Variable	Segunda-Feira de Páscoa	Easter Monday	Various places in central Portugal
Variable	Quinta-Feira da Ascensão	Ascension	Various places in central and south Portugal
13 June	Dia de Santo António	St Anthony's Day	Lisbon
24 June	Dia de São João	St John's Day	Various places in the north
29 June	Dia de São Pedro	St Peter's Day	Various throughout Portugal
4 July	Dia de Santa Isabel	St Elizabeth's Day	Coimbra
8 September	Natividade de Nossa Senhora	Nativity of Mary	Various places in south
21 September	Dia de São Mateus	St Matthew's Day	Viseu and Elvas
13 May and 13 October	Peregrinação para Fátima	Pilgrimage to Fátima	Fátima

GETTING THERE

By air

There are directs flights from all main UK airports to Faro, Lisbon or Porto, with major and budget airlines (see Appendix B for contact details); prices start from under £100 return. Porto is the most convenient airport for the northern region (Montesinho, Peneda-Gerês National Park, Alvão and Estrela). Lisbon is convenient for the central region (Sintra, Arrábida, and Aire e Candeeiros are within an hour's drive from the city, while Tejo and Marvão are about two hours away). Faro is ideal for visiting the southern region and the Algarve.

By car

It takes about 15 hours to drive through France and Spain from Calais (via the Eurotunnel or by ferry across the English Channel) to northern Portugal. It's a slightly shorter drive of about 12 hours if you sail to Brittany. Alternatively there are car ferries from either Plymouth or Portsmouth to Bilbao or Santander in Spain; it is then a 5-hour drive to northern Portugal.

Another option would be to fly to Portugal or Spain and hire a car; they are easily available at airports (see above).

By train
It's possible to travel from London to Lisbon via Eurostar, TGV and Sud Express, taking about 24 hours – plus another connecting train to Porto or Faro. (See Appendix B for rail operator contact details.) However, this is quite a tortuous and time-consuming way to travel and not necessarily cheaper than flying. With the emergence of budget airfares this has become the least favourable option.

Visas
EU citizens need an identity card only. Australian, New Zealand, Canadian and US citizens do not need a visa but must have a passport that is valid until at least three months after the end of their planned stay. Visitors from other countries should see the official Portugal tourism website for information (www.visitportugal.com; search 'visa'). For a visa application they should go to the Portuguese Ministry of Foreign Affairs official website: www.secomunidades.pt/vistos

TRAVELLING AROUND

Without a doubt a car is the most convenient way of getting around for the purposes of this guide, and access details are given for drivers in the information box at the start of each walk. The traffic is not busy except in major cities; however, Portugal continues to have the highest death rate from road traffic accidents in Western Europe, so drive carefully. There are different sorts of tolls: check with your car hire company or at www.estradas.pt

The Portuguese road nomenclature is varied. A national road on signs and in text is denoted by the letter

A moinho *(windmill)* on Walk 34

'N', but on some maps may be 'En' or just the number. Likewise, the smaller municipal roads may be denoted by 'M', 'Em' or just the number.

Trains run between major cities (Comboios de Portugal, www. cp.pt). Long-distance buses link most cities, large towns and many small towns (Rede Expressos – a national consortium of companies – www. rede-expressos.pt). There are bus services to locations near some of the walks in this book but they are infrequent with complicated schedules (details from tourist information offices), and an overnight stay is usually required.

WHERE TO STAY

Holiday accommodation is widely available in towns and even in remote villages. It ranges from hotels, guest houses, self-catering options, private rooms and youth hostels to camping grounds. Be aware that wild camping is not permitted. For a special treat, book a room in a *pousada*, one of the luxurious converted castles, palaces, convents or other historic buildings.

Prices in Portugal are very reasonable; an equivalent three-star hotel room or self-catering property is approximately €50 per night in Lisbon – cheaper in rural places – and prices start from about €75 even at a pousada.

The following websites may be useful in searching for and booking accommodation: www.airbnb.co.uk,

www.tripadvisor.co.uk, and www. booking.com. The websites for the national park, nature parks and the local municipalities are also useful resources, especially for rural places (see Appendix B). For the latter, booking might have to be done via the local tourist office by phone as some proprietors are not online.

For most of the routes in this book, accommodation is available in towns or remote villages near the start of the walk, as detailed in the 'Bases' section for each area. Public transport from a nearby town may be possible; more often access by car is recommended.

The standard of lodging does vary, and facilities tend to be geared more for hot weather: heating systems are often lacking, other than a wood-burning stove, especially in remote villages.

Practicalities	
Time	Portugal is on GMT (or BST during the summer). No time difference compared to the UK.
Money	Portugal uses the euro (€)
Electricity	220–240 volts AC

FOOD AND DRINK

Portuguese food is simple, unfussy, but nonetheless delicious. Eating out, fresh fish and meat (grilled or fried) are staple. Meals are very good value for money and traditionally substantial, suitable for people who've worked a hard day in the fields. You won't get many (or often any) vegetables, other than chips, as families eat greens at home whereas going out is a time to enjoy meat. Vegetarians are not particularly well catered for in Portugal. Note that *una dosa* (one portion) is for two or more people to share, whereas a *meia dosa* (half-portion) is for one person.

Unique Portuguese dishes include *feijoada* (bean stew with meats), *cozido á Portuguesa* (Portuguese stew, which varies across the country), *alheira* (a bready sausage), *salpicão* (a thick smoked pork dry sausage), *morcela* (black pudding), *linguiça* (spicy garlic sausage), *presunto* (ham, similar to Parma ham), *cataplana* (seafood stew – the name refers to the copper dish it's cooked in), *caldo* (a simple vegetable broth), *frango no churrasco* (barbequed chicken), *porco Alentejano* (pork with clams), and *migas* (crumbled bread fried with various additions). *Bacalhau* is cod, but in Portugal this is unlikely to be fresh, as they adore the dried, salted version, cooked in myriad ways. Every area has its own *pão* (bread), all hand-baked and wholesome, of which a particular recommendation is *pão Alentejano* (a rustic sourdough). In rural villages people get bread delivered to their front door, hung on the doorknob every morning.

Pasteis de nata (Portuguese custard tart) is a must, and if you have a sweet tooth the *doces conventuais* (convent sweets) will be irresistible. These delights stem from the time when the nuns used egg whites to starch their wimples; their solution for the surplus yolks was to combine them with sugar, various secret ingredients and a huge amount of ingenuity, enticing the congregation by appealing to their taste buds. Most towns and regions have their own special convent sweet.

The wines encompass a tremendous range of varieties, often using grapes not encountered elsewhere. You will find good table wine everywhere, with superb examples from all regions. The rich, powerful wines of the Tejo valley are particularly impressive. Port is only produced in the UNESCO-listed Douro valley, and *vinho verde* (literally meaning 'green wine', not referring to its colour but to its age: a young, refreshing, slightly sparkling wine) is only produced in the north. Setúbal is thought to be the oldest Iberian wine-producing region; its dessert wines are famed and were Richard II's favourite tipple.

EQUIPMENT

Good comfortable boots that you've worn before are essential. Sun protection is necessary at all times: consider using factor 50 plus a hat. While a single layer of summer clothing may be sufficient at lower altitudes for most of the year, it pays to carry waterproofs and extra layers of warm clothing in case of unexpected conditions and at higher altitudes. Proper walking socks of the appropriate grade are worth every penny. Wear long trousers for all walks as so many are overgrown or involve pushing through spiky bushes. Walking poles are advised: for protecting knees on descents, as a balancing aid when fording rivers, to lean on to help with ascents, to probe the terrain ahead, and to scare off the occasional dog.

A typical emergency kit would contain spare bootlaces, first aid kit (see 'Emergencies and safety', below), space-blanket/survival bag, snack bars, clean dry socks, insect repellent, tissues, Vaseline, battery bank, Swiss Army knife, emergency whistle, and torch.

WAYMARKING

Many of the walks in this guide follow established local and national trails.

Correct way/wrong way

Turn left/turn right

PR (*pequeno rota*) literally means 'small route', waymarked red/yellow.

GR (*grande rota*) is a long-distance route, waymarked red/white. The Rota Vicentina (Walks 35 and 36) is waymarked blue/green.

Be aware that the waymarking in Portugal is not always up to date; the marks may falter or disappear, or they may have been updated while the maps have not. It's best to follow the maps and route descriptions given in this guide, preferably in conjunction with GPS guidance.

MAPS

For Serra da Estrela, Sintra-Cascais, Arrábida and Peneda-Gerês, use Adventure Maps (www.adventure maps.pt). They are also available from Stanfords (www.stanfords.co.uk).

For other areas the best map is the Carta Militar de Portugal, published by Instituto Geográphico do Exército (www.igeoe.pt), but footpaths and rights of way are not included. The 1:25,000 version is available online or direct from IGeoE. The 1:50,000 versions are available from retailers such as Stanfords. Online maps are available (paid for) on the OutdoorActive hiking app.

There is reasonable coverage using m@pas online (mapas. dgterritorio.pt) at 'zoom level 8', but it is significantly more dated than the Carta Militar. Opencycle (www. opencyclemap.org) is useful and has some but not all footpaths, however

29

some footpaths on the map do not exist.

WATER

Tap water is drinkable in Portugal. Carry plenty of water when walking (*at least* 200ml per person per hour when the weather is hot). There are public taps in many towns and the water from these is reportedly drinkable unless there's a sign that says *água não controlada*.

EMERGENCIES AND SAFETY

Although the solitude is one of the major draws of walking in Portugal, patchy mobile phone reception means you may struggle to make contact in an emergency if you walk alone. Needless to say, if you do choose to walk unaccompanied it's good practice to inform someone where you're going and when you'll be back. There is no mountain rescue service: if you have a signal, call 112 for all emergencies (police, ambulance, fire service) and 117 for forest fire.

The most likely injuries are blisters, sunburn and bee sting, so in addition to the usual dressings, be sure to have antihistamines, painkillers and blister treatment in your first aid kit. Prevent blisters by choosing and maintaining your footwear carefully, and by responding to any discomfort

The footpath winds through the tranquil beech forest from São Lourenço (Walk 20)

as soon as you feel it. Clean and dry is the key to treatment if prevention has failed; apply some sort of blister dressing, and puncture with a sterile needle only if huge, leaving the skin as intact as possible.

Snake bite is incredibly rare as snakes avoid people, but they may bite if disturbed. Clean the site and avoid unnecessary movements, for example by using a sling if bitten on an upper limb. Contact the Poisons Information Centre (+351) 808 250 143 and go to the nearest hospital as soon as possible. However, there is no record of any fatalities as a result of snake bite. (See 'Wildlife' for information about the types of snake that might be encountered.)

Dogs

Dogs are everywhere in Portugal; many are quiet but some will mark their territory by barking. If they appear threatening, pretending to throw a stone at them is a useful deterrent. If bitten, rabies is endemic, so seek medical advice. (On the other hand, you may find yourself accompanied on walks by over-friendly dogs.)

River crossings

Many of the walks in the guide involve stream or river crossings. While in normal conditions these should pose no difficulties whatsoever (for the most part they are either shallow streams or crossed via purpose-built stepping-stones or bridges),

care should be taken after heavy rain, when crossings – or at least staying dry – may prove more challenging. Any particular risks are included in the information box at the beginning of the walk descriptions.

Health care

The EHIC (European Health Insurance Card) has replaced the E111 card, with which EU citizens are given access to temporary necessary state-provided health care for free or at a reduced rate. It does not replace travel insurance, which is highly recommended. This should cover repatriation and is essential for non-EU citizens.

USING THIS GUIDE

Information to help you choose a route that suits your capabilities is listed in the route summary table in Appendix A and in the information box at the beginning of each walk description. All times are pure walking times, with no allowance for photography, exploration, resting or eating. Throughout the guide, Portuguese words are italicised and there is a glossary in Appendix C. Places and features on the maps are shown in **bold** in the route descriptions to aid navigation.

Grades

Grading depends on distance, total ascent, ease of navigation and type of terrain, but as always is subjective.

	Distance (km)	Ascent (m)	Navigation	Terrain
Easy	Up to 8	Up to 400	Easy	Good paths
Medium	Up to 15	Up to 600	Mostly easy with a few difficult turns	Some uneven or muddy paths
Difficult	Up to 20	Up to 1000	Some areas with no landmarks and paths are not clear	A lot of uneven or muddy paths
Challenging	Over 20	Over 1000	Difficult	No paths/some scrambling

The given grades should be treated as a rough guide until you've walked a few of these routes, to compare with your own pace.

Leave no trace
This ethos is well embedded in the consciousness of most walkers. Take all your litter away with you, and under no circumstances should you light a fire: not only are they illegal for most of the year, but they also put the landscape at serious risk. Full rules for walking in the nature parks can be found on the ICNF website (www. icnf.pt).

GPS
GPS may prove highly valuable on many of the walks in this guide. GPX tracks for all of the routes are available to download free at www.cicerone. co.uk/889/GPX. Consider using a free smartphone app such as ViewRanger (www.viewranger.com), with roaming turned off and maps downloaded before the walk to avoid any extra charges (using the GPS function abroad is free).

A GPS device is an excellent aid to navigation, but you should also carry a map and compass and know how to use them. GPX files are provided in good faith, but neither the author nor the publisher accepts responsibility for their accuracy.

GPS coordinates have been provided for the start/finish points of all walks. They are Google compatible, and can be used on GPS devices (including in-car GPS and android GPS apps). If different formats are required, use an online converter such as www.directionsmag.com/site/latlong-converter

NORTHERN
PORTUGAL

*Rio Olo, which becomes Fisgas de Ermelo – the cascade
symbol of Alvão Nature Park*

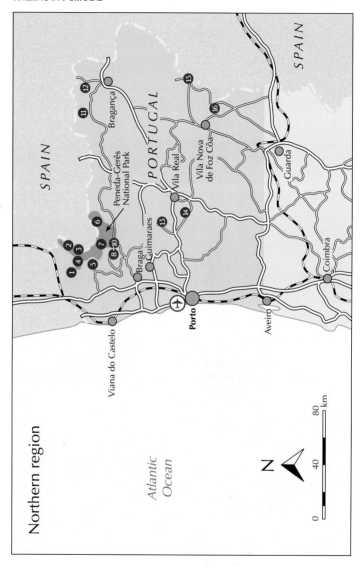

Northern region

PENEDA-GERÊS NATIONAL PARK

Walking along the beautiful calçada (pavement) towards Gavieira, with panoramic views of the mountain ranges of Serra da Peneda and Serra do Soajo (Walk 4)

PNPG is the only national park in Portugal. It extends between the two plateaux of Castro Laboreiro and Mourela, covering the mountain ranges of Peneda, Soajo, Amarelo and Gerês. The landscape ranges from breathtaking peaks and crags, via mountainous plateaued highland areas where livestock and wildlife graze, to lakes and waterfalls. Granite dominates the area with the presence of some metasedimentary rocks (shales) and deposits of glacial origin, such as moraines or erratic blocks.

Due to its diverse environment, the park provides habitats for a wide variety of wildlife including the roe deer (the emblem of the park), wolves and golden eagles. Serra do Gerês lilies are not found anywhere else in the world.

The list of highlights in the park is endless and includes the ethereal Sanctuary of Peneda (Walk 3), the megalithic monuments in Mezio (near Walk 5), the Via Nova Roman road (Walks 8 and 9), and a castle with superb panoramic views in Castelo Laboreiro (Walk 2).

The park's scenery, cultural heritage, history and architecture can be explored on the walks in this chapter; alternatively you could focus on

View of the village Gavieira at the bottom of the valley of Rio Pomba with the majestic mountain ranges of Serra da Peneda and Serra do Soajo in the background (Walk 4)

conquering the highest peaks of each mountain range – Louriça (1359m, Amarelo), Pedrada (1416m, Soajo; Walk 5), Carris (1508m, to look at the unattainable Pico da Nevosa in Gerês; Walk 7) and Peneda (1374m, Peneda).

There are five park gates with visitor centres providing advice: Lamas de Mouro, Mezio, Lindoso, Campo do Gerês and Montalegre.

BASES

Both Campo do Gerês and Villa do Gerês are at the park's geographical centre and have multiple accommodation options – although as the park is so large, driving distances for the outer walks will be up to 1½hrs. Many of the walks have both dining options and rooms available at the start town/village: Castro Laboreiro for Walk 2, Peneda and Branda da Aveleria for Walk 3, and Pitões das Júnias – the highest village in Portugal – for Walk 6.

WALK 1

Caminho dos Mortos, Real

Start/Finish	Capela do Senhor dos Passos, near Real (N42°00.658′ W08°22.938′)
Distance	12.5km
Total ascent	650m
Grade	Medium
Time	5hrs
Terrain	Mostly along old ways, uneven in places, a little bit of tarmac
Map	Adventure Maps Peneda-Gerês; Carta Militar 1:50,000 sheets 1-1 and 1-2, 1:25,000 sheets 3 and 8
Access	On the M503-1 between Merufe and Tangil
Parking	At start
Warning	Caution is required after heavy rain as the route crosses a number of streams, and in many places the water rushes along the *calçada* (stone-built pavement).

Caminho dos Mortos – 'Walk of the dead' – is a superb route despite its macabre origins. It follows the old ways, along which the dead used to be transported in ox-drawn carts to church for burial: if you look closely the ruts from the cart wheels are still visible. There is also a Neolithic burial mound now almost subsumed into the landscape.

The route goes through beautiful countryside, a couple of small villages, and in many places follows watercourses. Short enough to be completed before the heat becomes too oppressive, and incorporating a reasonable amount of shade, this is a walk that could be done in summer.

From the chapel walk south on the tarmac road downhill. Take the very first right-hand fork, and then by a small chapel/shrine (**Capela Sra dos Remédios**) turn right to walk on a *calçada*, which is the actual 'way of the dead'.

Walk upwards, over a solid stone bridge made of gigantic granite slabs, and past a beautiful old **watermill**,

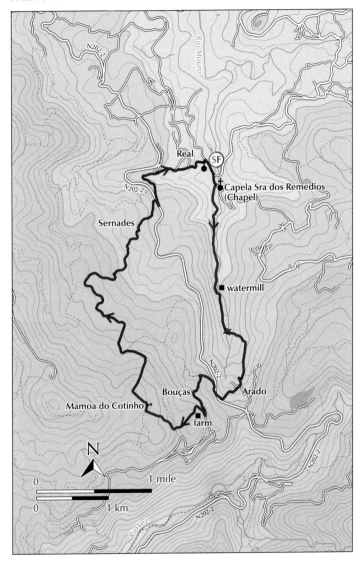

covered in moss. ▶ Shortly after the mill, the path, which has been next to the river, turns to the right (where there is also a turning to the left with amazing stepping-stones).

Follow the path and 10mins later cross over the river on a **bridge** made from huge granite blocks. Then ford a stream and 15mins later walk underneath vines in the outskirts of the village of **Arado**.

In spring, this whole valley is green with ferns and moss.

> The *enforcado* method of training vines at a height is commonly found in northern Portugal. It helps prevent fungal disease by raising the vines way above the fungal spores on the ground, which otherwise would get splashed onto the leaves by rainfall. The smallholders can also grow vegetables beneath them, an efficient use of space.

Reach a tarmac road and turn left, uphill, and then go straight over a crossroads to leave the village, heading up and south-west. Walk up the path, turn right at the large tarmac road, and then turn left in 50 metres. Go straight over a dirt road crossroads, then 350 metres after the tarmac road take a left-hand turn onto a cart track signposted for Bouças, with views of hand-built terracing down the Vale do Sucrasto.

Hand-built terracing still in use, with views down the Vale do Sucrasto

Once in the village of **Bouças**, turn left and then left again, staying on the tarmac road, and exit the village. After 250 metres is an acute right-hand turn: a cart track going uphill and nearly doubling backwards. Take this, and 200 metres along it take a left-hand footpath going uphill. Walk through the woods, along a path that is indistinct in places, to a **farm** where there is a fork. Go right, along a cart track, ignore a turning to the left and reach a T-junction. Turn right uphill, which is almost straight ahead.

Stay on this main dirt road until you reach a multi-way junction, then take the second right, counting anti-clockwise, going uphill through the woods. Reach a crossroads with another cart track and turn right, signed Mamoa. After 70 metres there is a very indistinct footpath on the right signed to **Mamoa do Cotinho**, a large doughnut-shaped pile covered in trees.

> **Mamoa de Cotinho** is a tumulus built around 4000BC, a collective funerary monument and a place of worship. The name means breast, and the dimple at the top shows that the structure was hollow and has now collapsed.

After exploration, retrace steps and continue down the rough, quite wide path, going straight over two crossroads with cart tracks. Some 15mins after the Mamoa, at the next crossroads, with a major dirt road (and excellent views of the valley ahead), turn left.

After 500 metres, turn right at a crossroads. Cross over a stream and take an easy-to-miss tiny footpath on the right-hand side, and then go right at the next crossroads. This footpath becomes a cart track. When the route straight ahead is so overgrown it can hardly be seen, turn left downhill, which is following the main track.

About 15mins later, at the bottom of this track, is a low wall and a T-junction with another cart track; go left here. Then at a T-junction with yet another cart track, go right. At the next T-junction go left downhill, which leads to a village called **Sernades** (also spelled Çernades). The

route underfoot goes from cobbles to tarmac, with vines *enforcado* overhead.

At a T-junction in the village turn left along Caminho do Paço, and then immediately fork right downhill. Reach a T-junction and go right, again downhill. Arrive at a tarmac road, turn right and then take the first left onto a cart track adjacent to terracing and vines, just before the road loops back to Sernades. This leads to another T-junction with a cart track; go right, down the valley to a quiet tarmac road, and turn right downhill. At the end of this is a T-junction with another tarmac road; turn right, and 5mins later return to the start.

Capela do Senhor dos Passos, the start and finish point of Caminho dos Mortos

WALK 2
Trilho Castrejo, Castro Laboreiro

Start/Finish	Igreja Matriz (main church), Castro Laboreiro (N42°01.820′ W08°09.506′)
Distance	17km; including castle: 19km
Total ascent	820m; including castle: 870m
Grade	Difficult
Time	6½hrs; including castle: 7¼hrs
Terrain	Almost all on the old ways
Map	Adventure Maps Peneda-Gerês; Carta Militar 1:50,000 sheets 1-1, 1-2 and 2-4, 1:25,000 sheets 4 and 9
Refreshments	Many hotels and restaurants/café in Castro Laboreiro
Toilets	Available near start
Access	From Melgaço (capital of the area), take the N202 to Lamas de Mouro, then take N202-3 to Castro Laboreiro
Parking	Available near start

This highly enjoyable walk follows closely what the villagers in this remote area would have used to get from village to village – and often still do. Now designated PR3 and waymarked red/yellow, it provides panoramic views of imposing mountains, some shade here and there, and an optional visit to a Romanesque castle on the summit of Castro Laboreiro, from where you can admire the whole route.

There are streams over the path in places so this might be difficult in winter, and navigation is tricky at times, making GPS particularly useful. The route may seem a little 'out of the way', but its rewards are plentiful.

You can visit the castle from here (see below), or save this until the end.

From the church go south past the town cross and *pelourinho* (pillory) to the tarmac road and turn left. ◀ Take the footpath to the right just before the new bridge and cross the impressive old bridge (Ponte Velha) with superb views of the falls with boulder-scoured cauldrons, and then rejoin the tarmac road.

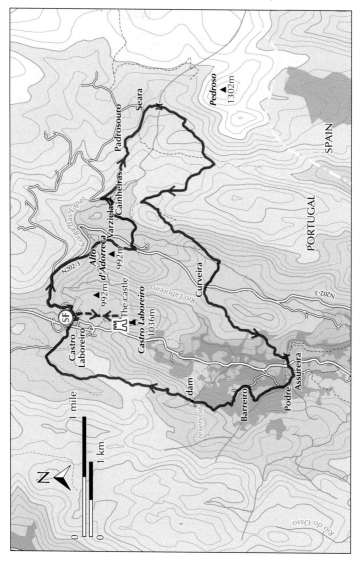

The Ponte Velha (old bridge) over the Rio Laboreiro on the outskirts of Castro Laboreiro

Walk along the tarmac road for 750 metres. Be careful not to follow 'PR Trilho Interpretativo' on the left, then take a right-hand turn signposted for Fronteira de Ameixoeira, following red/white/yellow waymarking. After 500 metres, take a pleasant footpath on the right heading down. Ignore a turning to the left, then cross over an old bridge leading to the village of **Varziela**.

At a T-junction turn right, and then 50 metres later, in the outskirts of the village, fork right along an old way. This leads to a tarmac road; turn left uphill and then take the first right-hand turn following signs for Cainheiras (immediately ignore a right-hand turn going to Bico). After about 5mins arrive in **Cainheiras** and walk past Capela da Senhora de Numão, then go through the village following red/yellow waymarking.

Capela da Senhora de Numão was built to celebrate an apparition that appeared in the nearby cliffs, credited with numerous miracles such as saving the lives of shepherds and their animals, and the healing of mouth ulcers. In 1712 Frei Agostinho de

Santa Maria, a religious writer compiling a list of holy sites of the area, said that it was so cold here in midwinter that the archbishop had to warm the Mass wine to prevent it from freezing solid.

About 500 metres out of the village, take a right-hand path off the tarmac and go over an old **bridge** then back onto the same tarmac road again. Take the second turning on the right 150 metres after the bridge, onto a footpath. Go up this path, then at a big fork go left and uphill. Stay on this path until the route is between two walls; go right at the next fork, leading to the village of Padrosouro. Don't go into the village, instead fork right just before it, staying on a cart track.

Continue along this enjoyable green path, through an oak copse, to reach the outskirts of the village of **Seara**. Take a right-hand turn just before the village, then take the very narrow fork on the right going downhill about 100 metres after the village. Cross over a photogenic **bridge**; about 5mins later the path becomes a little difficult to follow – there is a very old low wall and the path crosses over it. If you miss it, the path will just peter out upwards.

Ascend between two peaks, and then the path splits into three. Take the left branch, marked by cairns (although there are many other cairns, so caution is required). Turn left at a T-junction with a cart track, leading to a wide dirt road. Go right, downhill, following red/white/yellow waymarking.

Just over 1km along this path, in a wooded area with a summit to the left, take an acutely angled rough cart track on the left-hand side, nearly doubling back on the route. After 300 metres, between two summits, go right at an indistinct fork, ascending to the top of a crest to be greeted by a remarkable view deep down into the valley ahead.

Follow this excellent footpath down the valley for about 1km to a T-junction with a rough cart track and turn left with an old stone wall to the right. The route becomes a cobbled road; go straight through the village of **Curveira**, cross over a tarmac road and then immediately fork left onto a cart track.

Cross over a dirt road a couple of minutes later to walk along another lovely section of footpath through an oak copse with the castle of Castro Laboreiro visible to the right. About 500 metres later, take a footpath coming off the left of the cart track. Caution is required at the end of the copse; the route to follow goes right (west) and downhill (while the footpath goes straight ahead). Go over another impressive **bridge** after 5mins and turn right to head upstream. Cross over another stream via a little bridge, and then go straight over a tarmac road to a footpath heading upwards.

After a couple of minutes the footpath arrives at a cobbled road; turn left and continue uphill to the village of **Assureira**. The cobbles become tarmac, which ends in the middle of the village. Go straight ahead down a small footpath to a pretty river. Cross the river then walk on stepping-stones on its left-hand side, heading downstream, and take the next footpath going up on the left.

After 100 metres this leads to the village of **Podre**, where you continue straight ahead. Reach a tarmac road, follow it and go downhill, heading north-west. Just before a concrete bridge, turn left onto a footpath through the woods, walk past an old bridge on the right and follow the river upstream, keeping it to the right.

Cross over an ancient bridge to the village of **Barreiro**. In the village, on a tarmac road, fork right and downhill, and then go left at a T-junction with another tarmac road. Zigzag uphill and just before a building at the end of the road, turn right onto an old way lined with a massive wall.

Follow this straight ahead and uphill for 250 metres, ignoring the many turnings, and then at a three-way fork take the middle option, which is a *calçada* (stone-built pavement). Cross a beautiful double stone-walled **dam** 500 metres later and ascend an equally beautiful footpath to reach a T-junction with a dirt road. Go right, then ignore a turning to the left (this is PR Trilho Interpretativo, also waymarked red/yellow).

The path becomes cobbled 5mins later. Enter **Castro Laboreiro**, go straight over the tarmac road and back onto cobbled road, and follow signs for 'Centro', leading back to the church where the walk began.

To visit the castle

From the church, go south past the town cross and *pelourinho* to the tarmac road and turn left, then immediate right on a cobbled road, following a sign for the museum and castle. Walk up the cobbled road, past the museum to the summit (1036m) and **castle**.

> The Romanesque **castle** was built in the ninth century and Iron Age remains have been found there. Later occupied by the Moors, it was then retaken by Afonso Henriques (Afonso I, the first King of Portugal) in 1144. It was the scene of many a battle and became a National Monument in 1944. (Closed Mondays and on 1 January, Easter Sunday, 1 May and 25 December.)

Return by the same route after exploring.

Castro Laboreiro as seen from the castle

WALK 3
Peneda circuit

Start/Finish	Santuário de Nossa Senhora da Peneda (N41°58.456′ W08°13.395′)
Distance	24km
Total ascent	1200m
Grade	Challenging
Time	9hrs
Terrain	Granite stairs at the start, then proper footpath, some ancient granite shepherds' paths, some very rough dirt tracks and a short, quiet section of tarmac road
Map	Adventure Maps Peneda-Gerês; Carta Militar 1:50,000 sheet 1-2, 1:25,000 sheet 9
Refreshment	A selection of cafés and restaurants in Peneda; two cafés and a seasonal restaurant (July and August) in São Bento do Cando
Toilets	Main square in front of the sanctuary
Access	Follow signs on the N202 from near Soajo to Melgaço
Parking	Main square in front of the sanctuary

A long walk through some of the most dramatic scenery that Portugal has to offer. It encompasses an infrequently walked hidden valley with views that have to be seen (and earned) to be believed. It also provides the opportunity to see four different *brandas* (summer grazing villages) and a *santuário* (sanctuary). The *brandas* are still occupied: Branda da Aveleria is the most picturesque. All this is seen from the old shepherds' paths, hand-built from granite over millennia.

By following this route in a clockwise direction you will be heading up the steep granite steps at the beginning in the cool of the morning and mostly in shade, whereas the final section is gentler and in the afternoon is shaded by the mountain. The very last few kilometres are downhill along a road, giving your joints a rest after a day's walking on granite.

With almost no signposting throughout – despite being a combination of the official routes of Trilho da Peneda, a small section of Pertinho do Ceu (Walk 4) and Trilho de Aveleira – this is a walk where navigation would be difficult without GPS. The very rough dirt tracks and hard granite underfoot plus an ascent of over 1000m make this a difficult yet very enjoyable experience.

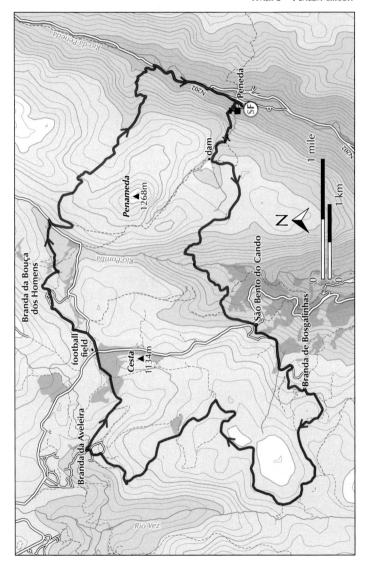

The monumental flight of steps leading to Santuário de Nossa Senhora da Peneda

The **santuário** is an interesting architectural structure – especially the stairs leading up to it with little chapels containing sculptures of 14 stations of the cross plus six more biblical scenes such as the nativity and the last supper. According to legend, Nossa Senhora da Peneda appeared to a shepherd girl in 1220, telling the locals to build a hermitage, although the current church was not completed until 1875. The annual Feast of the Lady of Peneda is in the first week of September.

The official start of the walk is to the left of the toilet block behind the sanctuary. Walk up the well-made granite steps behind it, waymarked yellow/white/red. ▶ Follow the granite steps to the top then cross the stream over a **clapper bridge**. Go right at a fork 100 metres after the bridge.

Arrive at a **dam** 1km from the start; do not cross it but follow red/white waymarking and turn left. The path then loops upwards and to the left away from the lake, rather indistinct for the next kilometre or so. This section is marked roughly with cairns, but if these have tumbled then head south from the dam, towards and through a small valley between two smooth hillocks composed of boulders, after which turn immediately right.

Next head west, with no distinguishing landmarks except the village of São Bento do Cando, visible in the distance across the valley. Follow sporadic red/white waymarking with some cairns; the path bears right across naked rock, heading north-west in the direction of some large wind turbines. Go over the crest of a hill, continuing to head north-west. After about 15mins, just before reaching a gully that blocks the route, follow the cairn-marked path as it loops round to the left and downhill. This path is manmade of vast slabs of native granite.

Reaching the bottom of the valley, cross the **Rio Pomba** via some large stepping-stones. Ascend through the verdant hidden valley lined with ferns and deciduous trees for 5mins until the path arrives at an ancient drystone wall. Continue with the wall on the left side of the path, following red/white waymarking. After about 15mins the path once again becomes granite, now waymarked red/white/yellow. This leads to a wide dirt track; turn left towards the *branda* of **São Bento do Cando**.

Arrive at the *branda*, head straight across the tarmac road and down a cobbled road to the back of the church. ▶ Turn right and right again, initially heading north-west. Continue along this narrow path to arrive at a dirt cart track; turn left (uphill). The path here is variously waymarked red/white and/or red/yellow.

There is a sign for Escala da Meadinha, a climbing zone on the impressive slab of rock under which the sanctuary lies.

Do not be tempted to make up your own descent; there are far too many sheer drops and impassable fractured rock fields.

There are two cafés nearby.

51

Verdant pastureland at Branda de Bosgalinhas

After 700 metres, arrive at the outskirts of **Branda de Bosgalinhas** and take the rough cart track heading right (the main path ahead has both yellow/red and white/red crosses). Follow this track to a gated field, then turn right along a steep uphill path between two drystone walls.

A *branda* is a high grazing village occupied by local people and their animals during summer. At the beginning of the colder weather they return to their *inverneira* – a winter village in the sheltered valley.

Reach a tarmac road, turn left and fork immediately right up a very steep concrete road heading south-west. This becomes a cart track, then you fork right at the next junction, with excellent views of the valley behind. Continue up the cart track, ignoring all minor turnings. There are some paddocks to the left, and a short section of granite track underfoot. Arrive at a T-junction with another dirt track after 25mins and head right (north-west); there is red/white waymarking on the left for GR Travessia das Serras da Peneda do Soajo.

Follow the dirt track for over half an hour to arrive at a major junction with a view of two sets of wind turbines. Turn left, which is north-west (the main path, which is the better travelled, heads right and east), towards some pine trees. The route winds its way briefly through a number of small pine copses, green and soft underfoot. As it heads down into **Branda da Aveleira**, ignore two right-hand turns (both dead-ends). At an attractively restored house called Teso da Costa, turn right and go downhill, following the main path into the village as it becomes a lovely stone-paved road.

Soon reach a T-junction with another stone-paved road, turn left and go downhill. Turn right at the next T-junction, with houses to either side, on level ground initially before quickly going downhill. Arrive at a multi-way junction with many signs for the various holiday properties nearby, and head downhill.

After about 50 metres take the unsignposted level footpath to the right of the road, heading south-east and leading to a stream. Cross over the stepping-stones, taking either of the two paths as they both go to the same place. Then take the right fork, continuing along the same path as before, with thick bushes to either side. (Ignore the left uphill fork despite it being wider and better travelled.)

About 10mins later reach a rough cart track at its hairpin bend and go left, heading uphill to a pinewood. Stay on the cart track until you reach a T-junction with another dirt track, still within the woods, and turn left, heading north-east. At the edge of the woods, arrive at a tarmac road with three options: take the middle one, going straight ahead and passing a **football field** to the left.

Continue on this tarmac road for 250 metres and take the next left-hand turn. This is a very quiet road only going to **Branda da Bouça dos Homens**. In the village, at a junction with houses called A Casrejinha ahead and O Ninho do Caçadora on the right, turn right and then turn immediately left. This is the only road out of the village and it rapidly becomes a dirt track, curving downhill.

Continue on this main dirt track for 1km, ignoring any turnings, until it meets a tarmac road. Turn right and after 20 metres go left up a beautiful granite path heading gently uphill for 1km (signposted Meadinha). The path is marked with cairns but no other waymarking.

Continue through a stunning landscape of jumbled and fractured granite for 1.5km, and then follow the path as it descends. Reach the end of this path after 1km at a large flat area and turn left along a short cobbled section which intercepts the main road. Head right and downhill for 1km to return to the *santuário* at **Peneda**.

WALK 4
Pertinho do Ceu, Gavieira

Start/Finish	Church at Gavieira (N41°57.462' W08°15.098')
Distance	8.5km
Total ascent	600m
Grade	Medium
Time	3½hrs
Terrain	All on excellent footpaths
Map	Adventure Maps Peneda-Gerês; Carta Militar 1:50,000 sheet 1-2, 1:25,000 sheet 9
Refreshments	Cafés in São Bento do Cando, plus a seasonal restaurant (July/August only)
Access	Head north on the N202 from near Soajo, then drive along M503 for 600m; turn right for Gavieira
Parking	On road

Pertinho do Ceu, 'Close to heaven', is a fittingly stunning little walk – especially satisfying if you've done Walk 3, as you can see its route from this one. Officially it is done clockwise, but doing it anticlockwise, as described here, makes the descent down the *calçada* (stone-built pavement) easier and safer.

The route includes a short section of the GR Travessia das Serra da Peneda e do Soajo, and as the name suggests, it does get very high up. Note that the route on some maps and websites is not correct – this route matches exactly the red/yellow waymarking.

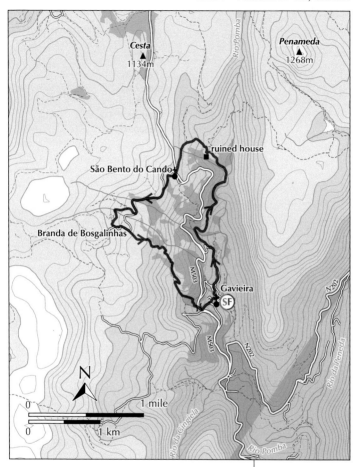

From the front of the church take the only tarmac road heading uphill and north-west, and then continue heading north out of town. ▶ Take the second right-hand turn onto a footpath, approximately 700 metres from the start. Go straight over a footpath crossroads after a further 100 metres, and then fork right to go to the river. Cross the

Rio Pomba is down in the valley on the right and there are some remarkable cliffs beyond that, on Walk 3.

55

river over stepping-stones and then follow the cart track along a pretty and shaded section, walking along the valley and heading upstream.

Ford another stream (with a gate next to it) and then ascend leftwards up the slope on an indistinct path. Pass close to the right of a **ruined house** where the path veers right and uphill. Along this section the waymarking becomes red/yellow/white. Meet a rough cart track after 500 metres and turn left, keeping a wall to the left-hand side. Follow this track for 500 metres to **São Bento do Cando**.

At the village, head straight across the tarmac road and down a cobbled road to the back of the chapel.

> This tiny and ancient chapel dedicated to **Saint Benedict** houses two holy images of him, and was an important site of religious pilgrimage. His feast day is still celebrated, although now it is more party than pilgrimage.

Turn right and right again, initially heading northwest. Continue along a narrow path, arrive at a dirt cart track and turn left (uphill). The path here is variously waymarked red/white and/or red/yellow.

After 700 metres arrive at the outskirts of **Branda de Bosgalinhas** and take the rough cart track heading right (the main path ahead has both yellow/red and white/red crosses). Follow this track to a gated field, then turn right along a steep uphill path between two drystone walls.

Arrive at a tarmac road a few minutes later and turn left, then fork immediately left, downhill. Follow this as it changes to concrete road through the village and past a very old thatched house. At the bottom of the village turn right onto a cart track (the main concrete road goes left). ◄

There is a paucity of waymarking along here.

About 150 metres after the village go straight ahead (the main dirt track goes off to the left). Follow the cart track downhill, not taking any turnings, to reach oak trees. Go right when there is a split (although both paths eventually lead to the same place), and along the descent

look north to admire the view of São Bento do Cando and the majestic peak of Meadhina.

Just over 1km later, towards the bottom of the descent with Gavieira in sight, take an easy-to-miss right-hand turn just before a shed to walk down by a wall. Follow this *calçada* under vines with a *levada* (water channel) on the right, then reach a tarmac road and turn right (if you missed the previous turning you will reach the same tarmac road but much higher up, so turn right).

Cross over the **bridge** and take the first left-hand turn, a concrete path heading down into the village. Take the next left-hand turn down a set of steps heading down to a stream. This takes you to the main tarmac road; turn left and follow this across a bridge heading towards the main part of **Gavieira** and the start point.

The village of São Bento do Cando with Meadhina in the background

WALK 5
Bicos and Pedrada

Start/Finish	Porta do Mezio (national park gate and interpretive centre) (N41°53.095' W08°18.834')
Distance	18km; including Pedrada summit: 25km
Total ascent	540m; including Pedrada summit: 780m
Grade	Difficult; including Pedrada summit: challenging
Time	6hrs; including Pedrada summit: 8½hrs
Terrain	A short section on tarmac, mainly dirt road, and *calçada* (pavement)
Map	Adventure Maps Peneda-Gerês; Carta Militar 1:50,000 sheet 1-2, 1:25,000 sheets 8, 9, 16 and 17
Refreshments	At start
Toilets	At start
Access	On the N202 between Arcos de Valdevez and Soajo
Parking	At start
Note	An ascent of Pedrada in poor visibility should be avoided, and even in good conditions GPS is advised.

This is a varied and interesting walk along an official PR, hence it is waymarked red/yellow (albeit infrequently). The optional non-waymarked ascent of Pedrada (1416m) is for adventurous walkers as there is no path at all, but it's difficult to resist the highest peak in Serra do Soajo. The main route does, however, include an ascent of Cabeço dos Bicos (1190m), which rewards with excellent views.

Along the way you're likely to encounter the local breed of cows – *Cachena*, with ferocious-looking pointed horns – plus feral horses and wolf traps, not to mention some splendid views and a stretch of *calçada* still in excellent shape.

The best seasons for this walk are spring for the impressive display of petticoat daffodil, or autumn, when the mists flow around the deciduous woods; ash, beech, birch and alder all underplanted with bracken.

The official route begins behind the interpretive centre, which doesn't open until 10am, so it's easier to walk up the road to the left of the centre signposted for Campisimo

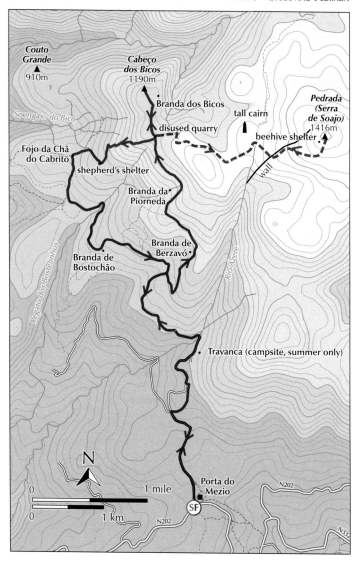

View from Cabeço dos Bicos

and Parque de Autocarrar. Walk past the parking area, ignoring red/white waymarking on the right and also the first red/yellow waymarking (which is the Mezio interpretive trail). Continue on the very quiet tarmac road until, 1.5km from the start, you reach a left-hand turning off the main road. Turn right here, heading along a wide path, manmade of large flat boulders. This route forks but they meet up again after only 100 metres.

Follow this attractive path for 10mins until the road is visible parallel on the left. The official path is straight ahead, but has been blocked with a locked gate so instead head to the road (no path) and walk uphill. Walk past a right-hand turn for Travanca (campsite), after which the road becomes a dirt track going downhill through more wooded land. At a T-junction about 2km from Travanca, turn right (the path to the left is the returning route).

Continue roughly north along the path, passing two ruined summer villages visible on the left: **Branda de Berzavó** and **Branda da Piorneda**.

The locals would have used this route to move with their possessions up to the *brandas*, which have not been used for hundreds of years. Low circular walls for livestock surround the tumbled-down remains of living quarters. In some *brandas* there are huge beehives, built large to protect the valuable honey from marauding bears, of which the last disappeared in the Middle Ages.

About 3km from the T-junction, the path turns sharply right just next to a small disused quarry, usually filled with water.

To climb Pedrada

Follow this right-hand path, now no longer waymarked, as it curves east and upwards with a tall thin cairn seen in the distance. Eventually it starts heading downhill, at which point Pedrada is visible ahead, the summit marked with a trig point and a radio mast.

Continue along the path, now heading gently uphill. About 1km from the disused quarry there is a long straight wall visible 300 metres to the right; leave the path when the stream is no longer present in-between the path and the wall, and walk to the **wall** (which is actually an ancient wolf trap). Look out for the tall thin cairn on the hill to the west – this is a landmark on the return.

Cross the wall, then walk parallel to it, heading uphill to an area where the stone is exposed underfoot. The wall crosses a gully and there is a **beehive shelter** on the hill up ahead; the gully is very steep to the north-west of the wall and the vegetation on that side is very dense, so curve right, around the undergrowth heading south-east to reach the end of the shrubbery and a flatter area. There are exposed areas of stone here and the shrubs are low, making it easy to get through.

Begin the ascent here, heading inexorably upwards for 300 metres until you reach the summit of **Pedrada**. ▶ From the summit, retrace the route back to the **wall** and path using the tall thin cairn as a landmark. Return along the dirt path until you reach the quarry and the point where you left the main route.

Try and memorise the route with care as there is no path, and this is the return route.

Main route

Head north on the official waymarked footpath between the quarry and a rocky promontory, through a small area

Beehive-shaped shepherd's shelter

of boulder field. **Branda dos Bicos** is to the right. Walk as far north as it is safe to do so, to be rewarded at **Cabeço dos Bicos** by a stunning view of the Ramiscal valley and waterfall. Retrace steps to the quarry, then turn right (west) and almost immediately arrive at a *calçada*.

Walk along until this gives way to a grassy area; from here continue in the same direction for less than 100 metres until you reach another, longer *calçada* heading downhill and leftwards. Follow it as it zigzags downwards.

This gives way to a rough track, a little indistinct but head towards the beehive-shaped **shepherd's shelter**, in front of which turn right and downhill. Stay to the left of a mixed copse of birch and pine until arriving at the large round structure of **Fojo da Chã do Cabrito**, which is a type of wolf trap.

From here turn left and downhill (keeping the wolf trap to the right), following a good path indistinctly waymarked red/white to a wide dirt track, and turn left. Continue along the main path for 400 metres, heading uphill (do not take a right-hand fork marked red/white), to another ruined village – **Branda de Bostochão**.

The path curves uphill around the valley, then head left and uphill at the only fork. Arrive back at the T-junction mentioned earlier (2km from Travanca) and turn right, downhill. Retrace steps to **Porta do Mezio** and the start.

WOLVES

This walk gives a fascinating insight into the relationship between man and wolf: for multiple generations there has been an ongoing war, with the wolf on the losing side. Human ingenuity to reduce the threat to self and livestock is demonstrated here with more than one method of trapping (and then killing) the ancient foe. The first is a straight wall: where the wolf would be chased by dogs, and then funnelled along the wall to low ground, above which the hunters would be waiting. The second is a structure with a one-way door, inside which a goat or other sacrificial animal was placed. This was still in use within living memory, and the one on this route (Fojo da Chã do Cabrito) certainly looks well kept.

See 'Wildlife' for information about wolves in Portugal today.

WALK 6
Pitões das Júnias and Capela de São João da Fraga

Start/Finish	Car park at Largo de Salgueiro, Pitões das Júnias (N41°50.456' W07°56.798')
Distance	12.5km; PR6 only: 4.5km; returning via Castelo: 13.5km
Total ascent	760m; PR6 only: 220m; returning via Castelo: 760m
Grade	Medium; PR6 only: easy; returning via Castelo: difficult
Time	5hrs; PR6 only: 1½hrs; returning via Castelo: 5½hrs
Terrain	Mainly footpaths
Map	Adventure Maps Peneda-Gerês; Carta Militar 1:50,000 sheet 2-3, 1:25,000 sheet 18
Refreshments	Restaurants, cafés and drinking fountains in Pitões das Júnias
Access	Take the M513 north from Covelães and after 5.5km take a left-hand turning onto M513-1. Pitões das Júnias is at the end of this road.
Parking	The car park on the right as you enter the village, off Rua Santinho
Note	In hot weather, consider doing the western part of the route first

The official footpath PR6 (waymarked red/yellow) in Pitões, at 1103m one of the highest villages in Portugal, is a lovely little walk but rather short, hence the added jaunt up to the ancient Chapel of St John of the Rock (Capela de São João da Fraga) on the summit of the same name (1165m). This latter section of the walk is not waymarked but it is regularly used by pilgrims and therefore easy to follow.

A return option via Castelo on an infrequently used footpath is great fun but navigation without GPS would be tricky, and it may be overgrown; if that doesn't appeal you can simply retrace steps to the start.

For a shorter walk you can follow just the PR6, completing a simple loop that nonetheless takes in some interesting features and good views.

From the start, head back to the M513-1, where there is a town cross, bus stop and a shrine. Here turn left (note

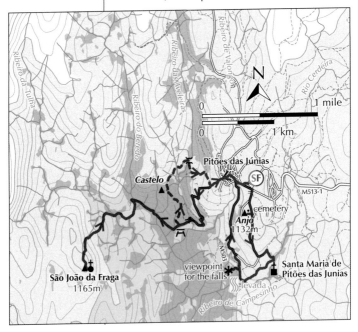

that the waymarking commences at the official start at the cemetery), and then take the first right along Rua Santinho, with a road sign for 'Mosteiro' (monastery).

After 250 metres, arrive at the **cemetery** and continue to walk along the tarmac road. ▶ The tarmac ends in a cobbled road; follow this to a wide area where the path forks, and go left following the 'Mosteiro' road sign (the right is signed for 'Cascata' (waterfall) – ignore this as the route goes there later).

The cobbled road becomes a cart track 50 metres later, then take the first right going downhill leading to **Mosteiro de Santa Maria das Júnias**, which is well worth exploring.

This **monastery** started as a Benedictine hermitage in the ninth century, hundreds of years before Portugal was an independent country, at the site of an apparition of the Virgin Mary to two hunters. The Romanesque church dates from the 12th century, when it was part of the Cistercian order, but is now in ruins following a 19th-century fire.

Mosteiro de Santa Maria das Júnias

The summit of Anjo is marked by a trig point just after the cemetery on the right.

The route turns off to the right just before the monastery opposite an enormous oak tree and granite table, going uphill quite steeply on the right of a low wall. Meet another footpath 250 metres later and turn left, signposted for the *cascata*. At the end of this is a T-junction where there is a *levada* (water channel); go right here. After 5mins, at a crossroads, turn left and cross a wooden bridge over the *levada*. Follow a wooden-stepped boardwalk all the way down to a **viewpoint** for the very high and impressive waterfalls.

Return to the main path and turn left to reach a cobbled road after 5mins. Turn left again, going downhill signed for Pitões. Capela de São João da Fraga is visible to the left across the valley: a tiny white dot on top of a summit. Follow the cobbled road for about 1km, all the way to **Pitões**. ◄

> Turning right here will take you back to the start if you want to do the shorter walk (PR6) only.

Proceed on the main cobbled road, heading northwest. Continue past two cafés and exit the village following signs for the chapel, now heading south-west. Take the zigzag cobbled road for 1.5km all the way down to the river, ignoring any turnings. Cross the **bridge** and ascend the rough cart track. After 200 metres arrive at a **picnic area** and head south-west (straight ahead).

After 5mins, cross over a stream on good stepping-stones and enjoy a beautiful footpath, mostly in the dappled shade of woodland. Continue along, ignoring a turning to the left signposted 'Ponte', and then cross over another stream, again with some good stepping-stones. On arriving at a footpath crossroads 10mins later, go straight over and follow the steep footpath to the **chapel** at the summit of **São João da Fraga**, and enjoy memorable views including Pico da Nevosa to the west – the highest peak in Peneda-Gerês.

> The **chapel**, dedicated to Saint John the Baptist, is so ancient that nobody knows how old it is. Every year, on the first Sunday after St John's Day, the locals from Pitões das Júnias follow a tradition, whose origin is also unknown, of climbing to the

top of the mountain in pilgrimage to the saint who protects the village.

Retrace your steps to the picnic area and then return along your outward route to the cobbled road and all the way to **Pitões**, back to the start.

Alternative route back to the start via Castelo

If feeling adventurous, turn left from the picnic area onto a cart track heading uphill. This becomes a very indistinct footpath with a wall on its right. Follow this wall for a couple of minutes to reach and take a left-hand turning – an old way going uphill between two walls initially.

Next take an easy-to-miss right-hand turning 250 metres from the old way turning. To the left is **Castelo**, a castle-shaped rock, not a castle (dangerous to climb). Follow the indistinct path marked only with some cairns. This reaches a stream after 600 metres; cross over the **bridge** and start ascending (this section may be over-grown). The route becomes a rough cart track, going up for 600 metres and leading back to the cobbled road that is the descent route from the village. Turn left, uphill, and return to the start in **Pitões**.

Pitões das Júnias, at 1103m one of the highest villages in Portugal, surrounded by the mountains of Gerês

67

WALK 7

Minas dos Carris,
Portela de Homem

Start/Finish	Portela de Homem (N41°48.503′ W08°07.831′)
Distance	21km
Total ascent	930m
Grade	Difficult
Time	7hrs
Terrain	Almost all off-road on a rough miners' track
Map	Adventure Maps Peneda-Gerês; Carta Militar 1:50,000 sheet 6-4, 1:25,000 sheet 31
Access	Take the N308-1 north from Vila do Gerês, following signs for Spain (Espanha). There is a tollbooth for access to the protected area (€1.50).
Parking	It is not permitted to park from the tollbooth until after the second tollbooth at the end of the zone, 100 metres from the Spanish border.
Note	A permit is required to do this walk as it is within a protected zone. To obtain a permit (free), contact ICNF by email: icnf@icnf.pt or tel +(351) 213 507 900 at least one week in advance.

Despite the inconvenience of arranging a permit, the 'Mines of Carris' trail is the classic walk of the Peneda-Gerês National Park, reaching its highest accessible point. Easy to follow, it's a there-and-back route with views at the top of Carris (1507m; not part of the official walk but added to this route for sheer enjoyment) that will leave you speechless. Being in a restricted zone, you are more likely to see the rare creatures of the park – roe deer, ibex and even wolves – than on any other walk without a guide.

The beginning of the walk is mostly in the shade of the mountain if you start early, and the route follows the course of the Rio Homem (River of Man), its glacial blue waters running over smooth boulders. In solitude at the top of Carris you might reflect that you've climbed considerably higher than Ben Nevis, without the crowds – and there's even the opportunity for a swim on the way down.

The ruined mining buildings at the top of Carris

Mining here began in the 1940s for tungsten, molybdenum and selenium. Despite being officially neutral, the Portuguese sold tungsten to the Nazis to build tanks and weapons during World War II. The mine was not completely abandoned until 1992.

Walk downhill from the parking area along the very quiet road. After crossing the bridge over **Rio Homem**, turn immediately left (the barrier is for cars, not people) and arrive at the beginning of the Carris path. ▸

Simply walk along the single-track old miners' path, where there are hardly any signs of human activity (this path excluded). There are two landmarks; the first is an old **curral** (animal pen) about 7km along, which has a bridge and a field with a beehive-shaped shelter. The second is at the end of the official walk, 1.5km later – a **disused settlement** built of brick and stone. Walk between the ruins and admire the magnificent views at the end of the path.

From here, **Pico da Nevosa** ('snowy peak') is visible to the north-north-east. At 1546m this is the highest peak in Serra do Gerês. It was previously closed but has re-opened. Authorisation is required.

There may be some tourists here admiring the waterfalls that are visible from the road, but few venture further than the cascades.

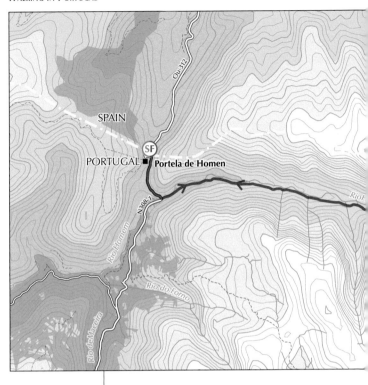

*One of the clean,
refreshing pools
of cool water,
Rio Homem*

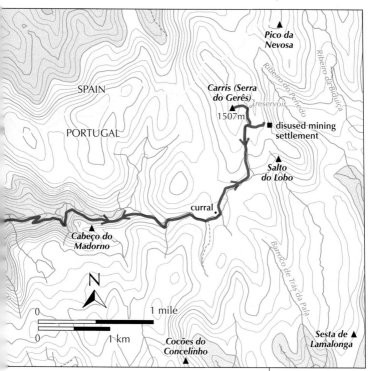

Walk back to the beginning of the buildings and turn right, leading to a **reservoir** with two dams. Turn left before the first dam and go to its west end before beginning the ascent. There is no proper path; just hop from rock to rock, heading west. After 200 metres (60m ascent), arrive at a trig point marking the summit of **Carris**, with yet more phenomenal views.

From the summit, retrace steps back to the mining settlement, and then back down along the miners' path. ▶ Arrive back at the road, turn right and return to **Portela de Homem** and the start.

On a hot and sticky day it's difficult to resist taking a dip or resting your feet in the refreshingly cold water of Rio Homem (but obviously only when it looks safe to enter).

WALK 8
Gerês circuit

Start/Finish	Near Albergaria restaurant, Campo do Gerês (N41°45.443' W08°11.576')
Distance	25km
Total ascent	1400m
Grade	(Very) challenging
Time	11hrs
Terrain	Almost all on rough footpaths, very steep and stony in places. A short (and very quiet) road section, with some dirt road towards the end
Map	Adventure Maps Peneda-Gerês; Carta Militar 1:50,000 sheets 5-1 and 6-4, 1:25,000 sheets 30 and 31
Refreshments	At start
Access	From Porta de Campo do Gerês (park gate), head north on N307. Where the road turns left to cross a bridge heading to the Albergaria restaurant, there's a dirt track heading north-east from the right on this corner, next to house number 850; park by the start of the dirt track.
Parking	On road close to start
Warning	Choose your time carefully: July and August are too hot and in winter there may not be enough daylight to complete the walk. Due to its remoteness and lack of waymarking, GPS is strongly recommended.
Note	The portion from Albergaria to Prado da Messe falls in a protected zone and a (free) permit is required. See Walk 7.

This outstanding – and very demanding – route incorporates the official Pé de Cabril walk, the Prados da Messe walk, part of the Geira Via Nova Romana and part of Trilho Águia Sarilhão (PR5). Despite (or perhaps because of) its challenges, for the seasoned and fit walker the sense of satisfaction is immense; the scenery is unsurpassed and the solitude and oneness with nature makes the perseverance well worth it.

Most of this walk is completely unmarked but lined with cairns, although some of these have been knocked down by horses/cows and sometimes there are cairns lining a different path, causing potential confusion. After Prado da Messe, the path is even more difficult to follow as it is not used by the locals. There is no shade on this walk until you reach the Roman road near the end, and although there are some springs for water, these may dry out in summer.

TO TURN THIS ROUTE INTO TWO CIRCULAR DAY HIKES

Option 1 (17km, 850m ascent, 6½hrs)

Follow the route as described below to **Portela de Leonte**, then head north along N308-1, a very quiet road for 2.5km towards **Albergaria**. Take a left-hand dirt track, which is the Via Nova, signposted 'Porta de Campo do Gerês' (if you reach Rio do Forno you have gone too far and should retrace steps), and then follow the main route description back to the start.

Option 2 (13.5km, 830m ascent, 6hrs)

Uneven paths and complex navigation plus significant ascent make this a difficult walk. Park at **Portela de Leonte** (N41°46.027' W08°08.810'), then follow the route description to **Albergaria**. At the tarmac road, turn left and head south back along 08-1 to Portela de Leonte.

Follow the dirt track, which becomes a wide footpath heading through the pine forest. After 10mins arrive at a fork and go left, then shortly afterwards at another fork take the right-hand, gentler uphill branch, heading south-west.

Cross a stream using stepping-stones 5mins later, then re-cross the same stream again onto a path. This leads to a gate to keep cows in (it might be closed with wire; after going through it be sure to close it again). There is an old wall to the left. Walk on, past many acacias, and a few minutes later the path curves left before ascending a steep, rough granite staircase. ▸

The radio masts at the top of Louriça – at 1359m the highest point of Serra Amarela – are visible to the north-west.

Take the difficult-to-see right-hand turn quite soon after Louriça comes into view, to a 1km-long but not-too-steep ascent leading to the Wall of **Penedo Furado**. After the wall, go downhill a short way, passing a spring with two animal water troughs embedded into the ground. Shortly after, there is a fork; go left and uphill.

After going downhill for about 5mins, arrive at a junction with two paths both marked with cairns; go left and uphill to arrive at a flatter area, **Prado Amarelo**. At a fork, go left leading to the shepherd's hut. The path then curves rightwards for about 200 metres before curving leftwards to ascend, heading north.

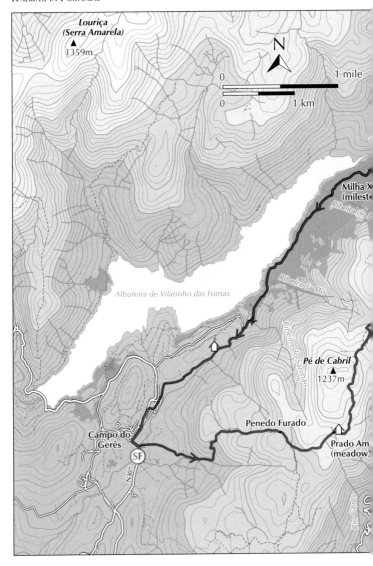

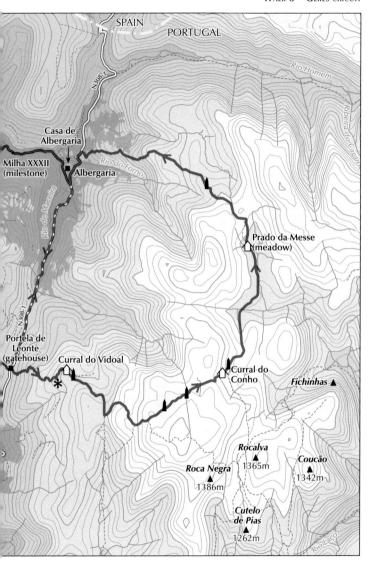

*Pé de Cabril in the
Serra do Gerês
mountain range*

After 800 metres of clambering upwards, including a slope of smooth rocks, the path becomes reasonably level and there is a large spire of smooth rock with a pointed top to the left: the summit of **Pé de Cabril** ('goat's foot mountain', 1237m).

Start descending along the path. Some 15mins further on there are three path options but they all lead to the same place. They cross expanses of smooth rock, with some cairns to aid navigation, leading to a grassy path. About halfway down this major descent there's a fork on a flatter area; go right (east). Continue until you arrive at a cart track, then turn right and walk downhill to the road. This is **Portela de Leonte**. ◄

The first of the two shorter walks deviates from the main route here, and the second of the two starts here.

> The name **Portela de Leonte** derives directly from the Latin meaning 'gateway to Leon'. The place is thought to be named after the mountain pass leading to Kingdom of León in the north-west Iberian Peninsula.

There's a tollbooth for cars entering the Mata de Albergaria (protected area). Cross the road, taking the path behind the tollbooth and heading upwards away from the road. This is the beginning of the Prados da Messe ('meadows of the harvest') walk.

The path is steep for quite a long way, surrounded by gorse and heather, whose aromas abound. It's mostly easy to follow as it's still used by the locals to access their *currais* (corrals), but there are some indistinct turnings. Follow the main path for just under 1km to a slightly flatter area – a spectacular **viewpoint**. ▶

About 5mins later in a stony boulder-strewn area the path is difficult to discern, marked only by intermittent cairns, but if in doubt head upwards. After 10mins arrive at an *abrigo* (shelter) at **Curral do Vidoal**, a flat area with a huge cairn. The path can't be seen here at all, and all the cairns had been knocked over by the cows that graze this area in summer. From the shelter, walk past the huge cairn, keeping it to the right and heading south-east initially. Follow the zigzag path upwards, then go across a relatively large level area, now heading north-east.

About 50mins from the *abrigo*, after a series of ups and downs, arrive at a junction with two paths, both of which lead to the same place: a flatter area marked with

Louriça is to the north-west, Pé de Cabril to the west, and to the south are row after row of serrated hills as far as the eye can see.

The stone-built shelter at Curral do Vidoal

an 8ft-tall **cairn**. Roughly 400 metres further along, pass another very tall **cairn**, and then walk on the right-hand side of a wall, heading down to a large, flat area via any of the various paths. From this flat area, head north-east through tall shrubs and across a dry streambed. After a short ascent, reach an area with a number of cairns, taking a zigzag, easy-to-follow path down for 10mins.

Arrive in a large, unexpectedly green and grassy glade, **Curral do Conho**, with ancient oak trees and in September huge numbers of autumn crocuses. Turn right at the shelter here, heading east towards a large cairn, and then curve left into a pass between two hills, now heading north. After about 2km, reach **Prado da Messe**.

Prado da Messe

Prado da Messe is a beautiful glade with a ruined house which was a forestry building in 1908. There is a shaded picnic area and shelter, which are still in use when the animals graze here in the summer. The name is thought to derive from an old dialect for 'meadow where rye was grown' – a tough grain perfectly suited to this hostile environment.

Go between the ruined house and the shelter, heading due north and uphill along an indistinct path unreliably marked with a handful of cairns. Be very careful here as there are two other paths also marked with cairns. The route you need to take goes uphill directly away from the back of the shelter and the picnic table.

Follow the indistinct path uphill through a gap between two hills and then ignore a straight row of cairns slightly to the right that goes downhill along the river valley. The route you should follow bears left on a curving path also marked with cairns, from which Louriça should be visible ahead after a while, arriving at another 8ft-tall **cairn** about 1km from the Prado. After this the path becomes slightly easier to see, heading north-west and downhill.

Halfway down more caution is required; ignore a gully-type path downhill and stay to the right and above it to reach, about half an hour later, the tarmac road **N308-1** at an area called **Albergaria**. Turn left and walk for about 500 metres; the road crosses **Rio de Forno**, then passes Fonte de Albergaria. ▶ Take the first proper dirt track to the right, which is the Via Nova, signposted 'Porta de Campo do Gerês'.

This tarmac road continues to Portela de Leonte and forms the connecting section for the two shorter walks.

From here the going underfoot becomes a lot easier, walking along a dirt road, past **Casa de Albergaria** on the right, after which the dirt track turns to the left across a wooden car bridge. The route now follows the course of the Rio do Forno, which then meets the Rio Homem, along a Roman road. Follow this long Roman road for 4.5km from the bridge, past milestones **XXXII** and **XXXI** (see Walk 9).

Cross the **Ribeiro do Sarilhão**, and about 200 metres after the river turn left onto a footpath. From here, follow red/yellow waymarking up the steep little ascent. When the path becomes more level, go past a **shelter** where the path curves to the left. About 10mins later the footpath metamorphoses into a cart track, which goes through a campsite, underneath a bridge, leading to a tarmac road. Turn left, and then at a T-junction turn left again, leading to the start in **Campo do Gerês**.

WALK 9
*Águia do Sarilhão and Via Nova,
Campo do Gerês*

Start/Finish	Porta de Campo do Gerês (park gate and visitor centre) (N41°45.013' W08°11.822')
Distance	16km
Total ascent	650m
Grade	Medium
Time	5½hrs
Terrain	Initially on road then mostly good footpath or dirt track
Map	Adventure Maps Peneda-Gerês; Carta Militar 1:50,000 sheet 5-1, 1:25,000 sheet 30
Refreshments	Many cafés and restaurants in Campo do Gerês
Toilets	At start
Access	Near junction of N307 and M533
Parking	At start

After an unassuming beginning along the road, this walk turns into a gem with excellent scenery and some history. It is composed of PR5 Trilho da Águia do Sarilhão, 'Sarilhão eagle trail' (waymarked red/yellow) plus a stretch of the Via Nova; you'll walk on the same stones that the legions of Rome would have marched over two millennia ago.

A superb trail to do in the height of summer, it is almost all in the shade, lined by native strawberry trees and the more invasive foreign silver wattle. There are stunning views of the Albufeira de Vilarinho das Furnas reservoir, as well as opportunities for a dip in or a picnic by the aquamarine waters of Rio Homem.

This is a route best done during the week, as Campo do Gerês gets very busy at weekends. Note that on some maps the town is shown as São João do Campo, or simply Campo.

> The 318km-long **Roman trade road**, built in AD80 during the reigns of Emperors Vespasian and Titus, used to run from Bracara Augusta (now called Braga, Portugal) to Asturica Augusta (Astorga, Spain). It is remarkable for having the highest

number of preserved milestones of any Roman road. It used to have 11 mansions (travellers' resting places), and plans are afoot to make the entire route walkable.

Facing the visitor centre, go along its right side to the road (some official trail leaflets are wrong at the beginning), then turn left heading north-east. Walk past an equestrian centre on the left, then another one on the right, and continue to follow the road as it turns left across a bridge. Take the next right-hand turn, Rua da Cerdeira, signposted for Vilarinho da Furnas and Parque de Campismo.

Here is the site of **Via Nova Romana Milha XXVIII** (Via Nova milepost 28). Take a well-signposted

map continues on page 82

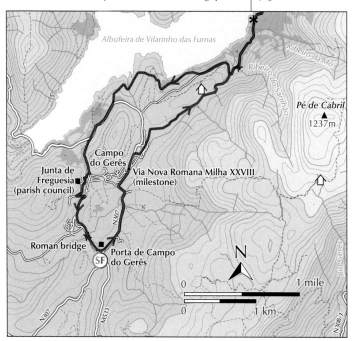

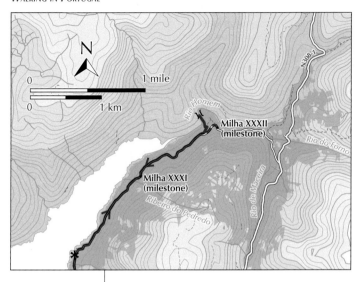

right-hand turn onto a cart track heading downhill just after a small plot of holiday bungalows. Walk along in the shade of trees next to a trickling brook; it is here that the beauty of the park becomes apparent, as you are surrounded by dense bush and steep-pointed fractured granite.

The cart track changes to footpath after half an hour and then goes steeply downhill, arriving at a dirt road. Turn right to head north-east, passing the yellow/red cross (the official waymarked path goes left).

Cross a **bridge** over **Ribeiro do Sarilhão**. There is a manned checkpoint 10mins along the dirt road, after which you are in the ambient nature zone (permit and toll only required for vehicles). Next cross the bridge over **Ribeiro da Mó**, just beyond which there is a phenomenal **viewpoint** across the lake. ◄

Early-morning reflections on the still waters are breathtaking, and it's a great place to swim in the heat of the afternoon.

Continue along for about 1.5km and arrive at **Milha XXXI** near **Ribeiro do Pedredo**. This is the first section of the Via Nova where the original Roman road is visible; there is a little stone bridge with a selection of columns.

After 1km there is a rough footpath on the left heading downwards. ▸ At the bottom of this path is a **bridge over Rio Homem**, whose amazing aquamarine waters gush over huge, gently smoothed rounded boulders. (The protected zone begins on the other side of this bridge and requires a permit even for hikers.) This is a fantastic point to sit in the shade and relax, next to the ice-cold water.

From here, retrace steps on the dirt road alongside **Albufeira de Vilarinho das Furnas reservoir**, to the point where this walk deviated from the official path, just south-west of the **bridge over Ribeiro do Sarilhão**.

The **Albufeira de Vilarinho das Furnas** is a huge reservoir formed in 1971 when the Rio Homem was dammed. The rising waters forced the total evacuation of the village of Vilarinho das Furnas, whose drowned ruins emerge when the reservoir's water level is low.

Instead of fully retracing the outward route, continue on the dirt road, now following red/yellow waymarking again. After 600 metres take a right-hand turn at a metal

To visit Milha XXXII with some beautiful surviving columns, continue along the dirt road for 250 metres, then retrace steps.

Vilarinho das Furnas reservoir

signpost for Geira, going down some steps onto a footpath. The footpath is clearly an old Roman road, very beautiful, tree-lined and shaded.

After about 850 metres, next to a drystone wall of water-smoothed boulders, turn right along a smaller track along the wall. ◄ Arrive at a T-junction on the footpath, turn left and uphill. Go left and uphill again at the next fork, and follow the main path to the tarmac road. Turn right, then take the first left turn, a tarmacked road heading steeply uphill.

Along here is another place where locals cool down in the waters during hot weather.

Continue straight ahead on the cobbled path at the top, leading into Campo do Gerês. Take the first turning on the right along a cobbled road past Abrigo da Geira, heading through the maze of streets and passing through the highest and westernmost part of the town. Go straight ahead to a T-junction, turn right and uphill (ignore the left-hand downhill path with an *espigueiro*/granary), then take the next left-hand turn.

Negotiating this maze of streets can be a little tricky; if in doubt, stay up high and aim for the **Junta de Freguesia** de Campo do Gerês (parish council building). Go past it then turn left and steeply downhill at a dead-end sign. Go down to a tarmac road, then turn right, passing another *espigueiro* on the right. Walk down the road and take a footpath to the left marked with an iron 'Geira' sign. Arrive at tarmac road 300 metres later, turn left then cross the **Roman bridge** and head back to the start.

Roman bridge in Campo do Gerês

WALK 10
Trilho dos Currais, Vila do Gerês

Start/Finish	ICNF office, Vila do Gerês (N41°44.249′ W08°09.516′)
Distance	10km
Total ascent	680m
Grade	Medium
Time	4hrs
Terrain	Mostly rough footpath, some cart tracks and a tiny amount on road. Steep and difficult in places.
Map	Adventure Maps Peneda-Gerês; Carta Militar 1:50,000 sheet 5-1, 1:25,000 sheet 43
Refreshments	Cafés and restaurants in Vila do Gerês, about 500 metres from start/finish
Toilets	In ICNF office when open, otherwise on main street in Vila do Gerês
Access	Drive through the town of Vila do Gerês (known also as Caldas do Gerês, Termas do Gerês, or simply Gerês), heading north signposted for Spain (Espanha) along the N308-1. Shortly after the town limits sign there's a left-hand turning signed 'Campismo Vidoeiro Gerês', leading to the ICNF office.
Parking	At start

Trilho dos Currais ('trail of the summer grazing areas') is a lovely little walk. Designated as PR3, it is another one that can be done in high summer, starting early to avoid the height of the sun, as it is mostly in shade. The route is well maintained and reasonably (but not consistently) waymarked red/yellow. The relatively easy-to-follow footpaths take you steeply up to explore the *currais* (corrals). The route encompasses some delightful scenery, including one of the most famous viewpoints in the area – Miradouros Pedra Bela, overlooking the vast reservoir of Albufeira da Caniçada, the town of Vila do Gerês and the glacier-scoured cliffs of Fraga Negra.

Curral (plural *currais*) simply means corral or animal pen. Some are still in use, where the villagers take their animals to the much higher grassed areas, both people and animals staying for the summer season in shacks. All the community shares the maintenance of the areas and routes.

Walk away from the ICNF office, back to the main road, then turn left and immediately right up some stairs. Go

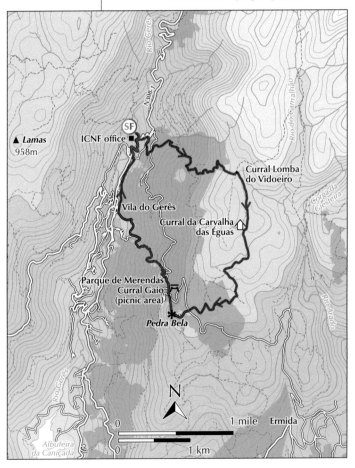

through the terracing to the cobbled road at the top and turn right along the rightmost of the various options, which is a tarmac road, heading along on level ground initially.

Curral Lomba do Vidoeiro with an impressive display of cairns

Take the first left-hand turn, after 100 metres, onto a cart track just before the tarmac road descends, and then take the first footpath on the left heading upwards. This leads to a tarmac road; turn left then immediately right along a cart track heading steeply uphill. Take the first turning on the right; this rough footpath is very steep but has the advantage of shade. Continue up for over half an hour until it meets a cart track, then turn left and uphill.

When the path begins to level out, becoming grassy and softer underfoot, there's a left-hand turning off this cart track into **Curral Lomba do Vidoeiro** ('corral of the birch ladder'), a plateau area with a myriad of cairns. In the middle of this, turn right onto a footpath and follow it for 500 metres to **Curral da Carvalha das Éguas** ('corral of the mares'). At the end of the field the path curves to the right and fords a small brook, which is followed by a lovely stretch through pine woodland.

A working curral – Curral da Carvalha das Éguas – with hundreds of goats, and two farmers having their lunch under the shade of the tree

Go immediately left at the next fork, with views of a hill topped with wind turbines across the valley. At the following fork go left along a cart track, on level ground initially, heading south-east. Then turn immediately right, heading west and downhill. The track becomes a footpath through pine woodlands, still heading downhill.

Continue along the path into a forest glade, then take the leftmost track heading south-west. After 250 metres arrive at a T-junction with a cart track and turn left, heading south. This leads to a tarmac road with three possibilities; take the middle one, signposted for Pedra Bela. Continue along the road for 300 metres to arrive at **Pedra Bela Miradouro**.

There are three **viewpoints** here, and it is well worth taking some time to explore. The best of the three is arguably Miradouro Velho (834m), with magnificent views down to the town of Vila do Gerês and a good look at Fraga Negra on the other side of the valley. There are also shaded picnic tables.

From Pedra Bela, near a large boulder with a metal inscription, turn directly into the woods heading north and downhill. This path is indistinct; just walk downhill and it will become apparent. Arrive at a tarmac road after 300 metres and go directly across it to another footpath heading downhill. Follow this for 100 metres to another tarmac road, where there are some more picnic tables in shade and a spring/fountain at **Parque de Merendas Curral Gaio**.

View of the Serra do Gerês and Albufeira da Caniçada from Pedra Bela

Go right and downhill, then take a left-hand footpath which just cuts a corner off the road. ▶ Once back on the road, follow it down for 50 metres and then take a left-hand turn onto a track heading away from the road. This is a rough cart track that zigzags steeply downhill to a tarmac road next to a *lavadouro* (communal clothes-washing place).

Vila do Gerês is now visible below.

Continue downhill along the tarmac road for about 250 metres to arrive at a junction with a 'no entry' sign dead ahead and a 'one way' sign to the left. Turn right, which is mostly level and just above the majority of the town. This becomes a gently ascending road and arrives

89

Serra do Gerês with Villa do Gerês below, viewed from Pedra Bela Miradouros

at a fork after about 1km; take the left-hand path, which is initially level before going uphill slightly.

The path eventually becomes a private driveway; continue and arrive at a cobbled road, then turn left and go downhill to the main road. Turn right, uphill, and walk past the town limits sign for Vila do Gerês along the main road, signposted for Spain (Espanha): this leads back to the **ICNF office** in less than 500 metres. Alternatively, walk through the little park by the town limits sign, on the left-hand side.

MONTESINHO NATURE PARK

Ploughing the fields the old-fashioned way involves the whole family; in the background is an agrarian landscape of lower-level mountains

Montesinho Nature Park is situated in the north-eastern part of Portugal in the region of Trás-os-Montes Terra Fria – literally meaning 'cold land behind the mountains', where the locals jovially describe the climate as 'nine months of winter and three months of hell'. The park encompasses the mountains of Serra de Montesinho (a granite massif extending to Spain) and Serra da Coroa, with a diversified landscape ranging from 1200–1400m high mountains – where it usually snows from December to March – to irrigated fields and pastures of ancient agricultural practice in the open valleys, interspersed with hamlets of granite houses roofed in slate.

This is a little-known and almost untouched gem populated with ancient woods: the symbol of the park is the chestnut flower.

BASES

Bragança is the nearest major town. It has a full range of facilities and is within easy driving distance of all of the walks in this chapter. Montesinho (Walk 12) also has hotels and cafés.

WALK 11
Trilho da Calçada, Moimenta

Start/Finish	Town square, Moimenta (N41°57.050′ W06°58.474′)
Distance	8km
Total ascent	350m
Grade	Easy
Time	3hrs
Terrain	All on good paths
Map	Carta Militar 1:50,000 sheet 3-II, 1:25,000 sheet 11
Refreshments	Café near start
Access	Take the N308 from Bragança, and just outside Dine follow signs to Moimenta, which is roughly another 13km away. Drive through the town until you reach a modern square next to what used to be the primary school.
Parking	At start

The official PR7 Calçada ('Pavement') route is a lovely little walk with all the necessary ingredients of a short hike: a decent ascent, a viewpoint, open hills, shaded woods filled with wild roses and ferns, plus some history in the form of the *calçada* and medieval bridge. The Rio Tuela is peaceful and attractive, and below the bridge look out for many *marmitos* (boulder-scraped holes). All of this contained within a walk that can be completed in a morning.

> **'Calçada'** translates as pavement, road or sidewalk. Here it refers to the old stone paths, often granite, found throughout Portugal. They were built using Roman techniques and are usually about 1.5 metres wide. They formed a vital part of the transport infra-structure before the advent of tarmac roads, and were used by villagers, merchants and pilgrims over the centuries. The grooves left by cart wheels can often still be seen.

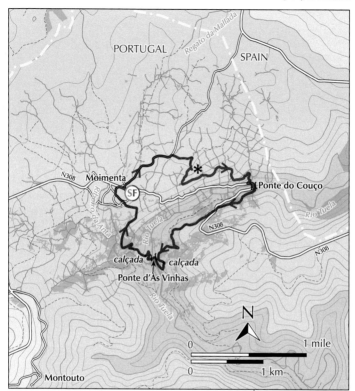

From the start point, exit from the north-west corner of the square (between the old school and the Junta de Freguesia) and head north on tarmac road. Take a right-hand cart track 1km out of town, signposted 'Miradouro', and then take the first right to the **viewpoint**, which has a scaffolding-like structure.

After admiring the views, continue on the footpath heading south-west downhill back towards Moimenta. After 250 metres, at a T-junction with another footpath, go left, heading away from Moimenta and down the valley. Just under 1km later take an indistinct footpath heading off

93

to the right (with some waymarks and cairns), leading to a wooded area where there is a T-junction. Go right to reach a tarmac road, then turn left (downhill) for 100 metres.

Cross over the new bridge (**Ponte do Couço**) and then immediately take a left-hand turn going uphill (the level one is a dead-end). Continue on this rough cart track, ignore a turning to the left, and then head straight over the tarmac road to walk on a better-used cart track.

About 1km from the tarmac road, take a very faint cart track on the right-hand side, nearly doubling back on the route. Follow this cart track for just over 500 metres, ignoring all turnings, and arrive at a T-junction with a more major cart track. Turn right and downhill for 250 metres, leading to the medieval **Ponte d'Às Vinhas** ('Bridge to the Vineyards') with some *calçada* before it.

Cross over the bridge and continue on the *calçada* as it zigzags uphill. Turn right 500 metres after the bridge to go uphill, still following the *calçada*. This leads back to the village of **Moimenta** in 1km.

Walk past the church to a T-junction; go left and at the end of that road is a café where the route turns right. Follow the main cobbled road until it meets a tarmac road and turn right, leading back to the start.

The calçada and Ponte d'Às Vinhas

WALK 12

Montesinho summits

Start/Finish	Village square, Montesinho village (N41°56.358′ W06°45.904′)
Distance	22.5km; following PR3 only: 7km
Total ascent	680m; following PR3 only: 300m
Grade	Difficult; following PR3 only: easy
Time	7½hrs; following PR3 only: 2½hrs
Terrain	All off-road; a mixture of dirt roads, cart tracks and footpaths
Map	Carta Militar 1:50,000 sheet 3-II, 1:25,000 sheets 11 and 12
Refreshments	Two cafés in Montesinho village
Access	From Bragança, head north on N103-7 for about 17km. Turn left onto M1026 and the village is at the end of this road.
Parking	Anywhere reasonable within the village
Note	The route follows some unnamed and unwaymarked paths; GPS is recommended.
Warning	Avoid this route in the height of summer

An outstanding walk involving a significant ascent, the two highest peaks in Montesinho Nature Park, two dams, a high chance of seeing goshawks, and a deserted hamlet. The route combines PR3 Porto Furado, a section of GR and some lesser-frequented paths.

The two summits (unnamed, 1486m and Bouça, 1437m) have different views, both exceptional; they require some stamina but the rewards are plentiful. An easy, shorter alternative would be to walk just the PR3 as a circular route, ascending through chestnut groves to the main reservoir that supplies the village and environs.

Start by heading north-east on Rua da Cimo in Montesinho (may be spelled Montezinho on some maps), following the red/yellow waymarkings. Go past some beautiful houses, bedecked with flowers, and almost immediately begin a steep ascent along a dirt track.

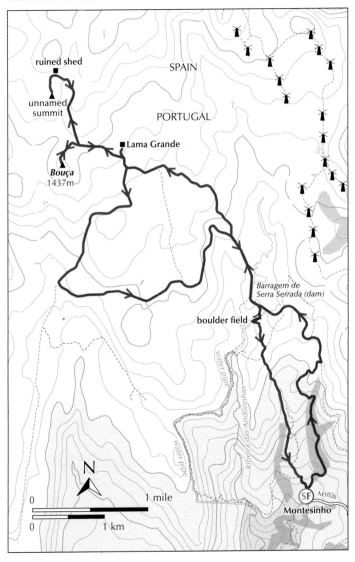

ruined shed

unnamed
summit

Bouça
1437m

■ Lama Grande

SPAIN

PORTUGAL

Barragem de
Serra Serrada (dam)

boulder field

water pipe

water pipe

Ribeira das Andorinhas

N

0   1 mile

0   1 km

(SF) *M1026*
Montesinho

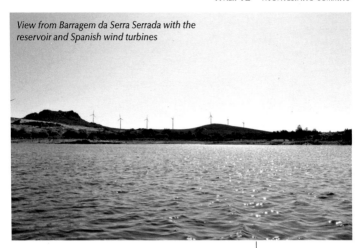
View from Barragem da Serra Serrada with the reservoir and Spanish wind turbines

Continue on the main track for 2.5km to a T-junction with a more travelled dirt track, then turn left heading north. (The wind turbines visible ahead are all in Spain as this is very close to the Spanish-Portuguese border.) Follow the main waymarked track for 1.5km to arrive at the **Barragem da Serra Serrada dam**, and walk across it. ▶

Continue on the main track, following red/white GR waymarkings, as it goes around the left-hand side of the reservoir. Ignore turnings to the left; the path then curves gradually away from the lake. Take a waymarked right-hand turn 1km after the dam onto a rough cart track surrounded by bracken and heathers (this is where the return route is encountered). Just 150 metres later, take a waymarked footpath to the left and follow this through the boulder-strewn landscape. The route turns slightly left to go across a small gully, after which it turns rightwards.

Arrive at a crossroads with a cart track 250 metres later and continue straight across, then curve left immediately. Walk along an indistinct path along a sparse line of silver birches; the path then joins a dirt track. This becomes a gorgeous shady track lined for about 500

You can cut short the route by turning left here to pick up the red/yellow and red/white waymarked PR3 path back to Montesinho.

Ruined house built using boulders at Lama Grande

metres with more silver birches to either side, leading to **Lama Grande**.

> **Lama Grande** translates as 'big mud'. This deserted hamlet is the highest village in the nature park. There are two houses to the right, which used to be holiday accommodation managed by the park authority but they have now lapsed into disrepair. The large one is built with gigantic boulders acting as an integral part of its structure.

The official (well-waymarked) trail is to the left, but our route goes right to explore the deserted hamlet and to conquer the two summits. To the right of a large square paddock there is a row of six ruined terraced farm workers' cottages, behind which is the path to the summits. To the right, about 150 metres away, are the two ruined houses. After exploring Lama Grande, take the summits path, heading west.

After 600 metres arrive at a fork (to be returned to later) and go right, heading north-west. The path at times is a little indistinct; head towards a **ruined brick shed-like**

structure. At the shed there is no true path from herein on, so just head upwards in a south-west direction to reach the **unnamed summit**.

> This unnamed summit is thought by some locals to be **Montesinho Peak**, the highest peak in the region. Curiously, Bouça (the second highest) has a trig point on it, whereas this has nothing but a small cairn. To add further confusion, there's another Montesinho Peak (1155m) much further south.

Retrace the route to the fork encountered earlier. Now take the other fork, heading west towards a peak marked with a white trig point. After 100 metres take the tractor track heading left for 350 metres to **Bouça** summit (1437m). ▶

Return to **Lama Grande** and then follow the red/white waymarked trail heading south. Go right at the next fork (after about 500 metres) and continue to follow red/white waymarking, due west. Follow this track for 1.5km to a T-junction with a major dirt road and leave the GR, turning left to head uphill and south-east. Ignore

From the top there are panoramic views of a huge new dam not on any maps, and of Lama Grande.

View from Bouça summit, with the new dam/reservoir being constructed

any turns until you reach **Barragem da Serra Serrada**. Just before the dam, turn right to head south.

You are now back on PR3.

◄ Follow a narrow walking path which is well way-marked with red/yellow and red/white. Pass to the left-hand side of some large boulders, then underneath a **water pipe**. Cross a stream 150 metres below the dam in the wetlands via a clapper-gate **bridge** of huge granite slabs. Shortly after this take a right-hand turn, heading through the brush.

Enter a **boulder field** – the first of which has a hole that could be crawled through – and take a left-hand turn through a narrow gap between two gigantic boulders. Then go uphill for a short distance over smooth rock, to arrive at a dirt road. Turn right, downhill, and 100 metres later take a small path turning off on the left.

Continue to follow the path, now on the left of a dried-out riverbed full of green bushes and trees. Cross over this via another clapper-gate bridge; here the path becomes a little indistinct, but head south. The path leads to a tractor track with turnings in three directions; take the middle one heading to **Montesinho** and follow it for 5mins back to the start.

AROUND ALVÃO NATURE PARK

Castro Castroeiro with Mondim do Basto in the background (Walk 13)

Alvão is known as the little brother of Peneda-Gerês National Park, with smaller, gentler rolling hills. It is located in the transition zone between the Minho and Tras-os-Montes regions, straddling the Serra do Alvão and Serra do Marão.

Rio Olo rises on the granite massif, and just before the village of Ermelo an imposing quartzite barrier forces the river to carve through it, giving rise to a spectacular 300-metre-drop waterfall, the symbol of the park. Look out for the so-called 'granite balls', huge boulders strewn around the terrain. Look out also for the special breed of cow, the *Maronesa*, that looks like the extinct auroch.

There are plenty of walks within the park (see www.icnf.pt), although the two routes provided here happen to be just outside of it. However, a visit to the park is highly recommended, as is time spent exploring the villages (Ermelo, Lamas de Olo and Arnal) in order to admire their typical rural architecture.

BASES

The towns of Vila Real and Mondim de Basto (the start point for Walk 13) are situated on either side of the park, making them convenient places to stay. They both have a full range of accommodation and dining options, as well as shops and other facilities.

WALK 13
Senhora da Graça, Mondim de Basto

Start/Finish	Roundabout, Mondim de Basto (N41°24.635′ W07°57.075′)
Distance	14.5km
Total ascent	850m
Grade	Difficult
Time	6hrs
Terrain	Mainly on granite pilgrims' paths, plus a section of road and dirt track
Map	Carta Militar 1:50,000 sheet 10-4, 1:25,000 sheets 86 and 87
Refreshments	Many cafés and restaurants in Mondim de Basto; café/restaurant at Monte Farinha summit; tap to refill water bottles next to sanctuary
Toilets	At summit
Access	The start-point is near the roundabout (the junction between Largo do Conde de Vila Real and Avenida da Igreja) just below the woodland park Parque Forrestal in Mondim de Basto.
Parking	On road near start

Although this is outside Alvão Nature Park, PR1 Senhora da Graça ('Path of the Lady of Grace') is included here as it is nearby, and the summit of Monte Farinha is visible from most areas of the park (and vice versa). The pilgrims' way with a huge ascent leads to Santuário de Nossa Senhora da Graça, with a small diversion to a fascinating Iron Age settlement en route.

The views from the top alone make the effort worthwhile, and the navigation and terrain are fairly straightforward throughout. The official circular path is recommended here rather than an out-and-back route, as it allows a gentler descent and provides slightly different views; however, the long section on road means that a return by the outward route, although steeper, may be an attractive option (12km, 700m ascent, 5hrs). The walk is intermittently waymarked red/yellow.

The walk begins at a noticeboard beside the roundabout. Walk along the pavement with a big retaining wall on

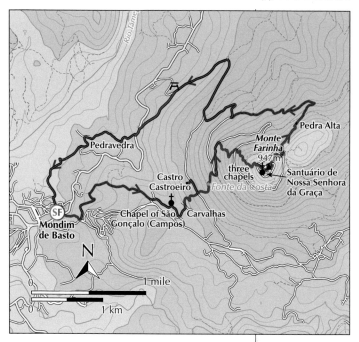

the right-hand side, heading north-east. Then take a right-hand turn, going upwards on a granite footpath. Arrive at a cobbled road 250 metres later and turn left uphill, then immediately left again, back on a tarmac road. This then becomes a cart track.

Don't take any side tracks; just follow the main path. ▶ At a major fork 10mins later, turn right and uphill. About 300 metres after the major fork, take a right-hand turn uphill on an uneven footpath. There's a double-walled path that is so overgrown it's no longer used; the route is on the logging path adjacent to it.

Arrive at a tarmac road at a bend 400 metres later, head left and downhill, and then turn right at the next junction. Continue along the road and pass the **Chapel of São Gonçalo** on the left in the village of Campos.

The *santuário* is visible at the top of the summit and looks a long way up!

Autumnal colours of enforcado (high) trained vines, unique to Portugal

When the buildings start to thin out, take a left-hand downhill turn at a blue tiled picture of Jesus. This road becomes a stone track, metamorphosing to a cobbled road to the small village of **Carvalhas** some 200 metres further along. At a T-junction, turn left and then immediately right up a steep stone footpath with an *espigueiro* (granary) on the right. Once past the last building in Carvalhas, take a right-hand steep granite footpath and walk up to a busy main tarmac road. The route is across the road, but it's worthwhile following the sign to **Castro Castroeiro**, 200 metres along the road to the left.

This is the **archaeological site** of the remains of an Iron Age settlement. Built on the site of an earlier Bronze Age settlement, as evidenced by concentric circular rock carvings, it had formidable double-walled fortifications.

After exploration, return to the route and go uphill. Take a well-signposted right-hand turn after a few metres of ascent, along a good granite path. Arrive at a crossroads with a logging track, go left and then immediately right (a staggered junction). **Fonte da Costa**, a fountain with springwater and a shaded area for a break, is 50 metres further on.

Pass the fountain and continue to a tarmac road, then turn right and uphill. After about 500 metres take a footpath on the right marked with huge granite boulders. This leads to another tarmac road (the same one that is zigzagging upwards); cross straight over and ascend the granite staircase.

There's a small **chapel** (the first of three) with a nativity scene; the route is then crossed by a cart track. Turn right up the cart track for 10 steps, then turn left uphill. Pass another **chapel** – known as the 'middle chapel' and dedicated to Our Lady's cousin St Elizabeth – just before tarmac road. Cross the road and take the granite steps to the right, leading to the third **chapel** (Annunciation). Continue ahead and arrive at the road again, turn right then curve to the left, taking the steps up to the **sanctuary** on the summit of Monte Farinha. ▶

The santuário is the fourth building constructed on this site and dates from 1775.

After exploring the sanctuary and admiring the views, take the stairs behind the main chapel down to a big open space, then go down another set of stairs on the far right corner. This leads to a stone road; follow this downhill and very soon arrive at a tarmac road, then go right and downhill. Just before the 'P' parking sign, turn left down some steps and shortly arrive at a tarmac road. Turn right (downhill) and immediately left into a parking area. On the left of the parking area take a signposted path going downhill with some stairs leading to a cart track, then take an unsignposted right-hand turn after a few metres and zigzag down the path.

After just over 500 metres pass **Pedra Alta**, a tall white-painted megalith, then cross a dirt road to continue on the route. The footpath meets a cart track; turn

Santuário de Nossa Senhora da Graça

105

left and go downhill. Continue straight ahead (ignore a right-hand turn after about 500 metres, although it looks well-travelled), then turn right at a tarmac road. Walk along the road (behind the crash barrier when possible) to a **picnic area** on the right with a road sign marking the way to the A7.

Here, take the left-hand fork (which is straight ahead). This joins another bigger tarmac road at a junction with a petrol station across the road. Bear left and continue downhill. Just after the first building on the right, 100 metres after the petrol station, turn right into a cobbled road, finally leaving the big tarmac road. This leads to the village of **Pedravedra**, and becomes a quiet village tarmac road. At the next T-junction, turn right and go downhill. At a five-way junction take the leftmost, indistinctly signposted option, heading downhill.

At the next T-junction, 500 metres later, go left and downhill to arrive at a wide fork with a small river at the bottom. Take the left fork uphill and go up the staircase on the right-hand side of the bus station in **Mondim de Basto**. Cross the road and arrive back at the start.

WALK 14
Marão summit

Start/Finish	Capela de Soutelo (chapel) in Soutelo (N41°15.511′ W07°51.592′)
Distance	13km
Total ascent	860m
Grade	Difficult
Time	5hrs
Terrain	All on cart tracks
Map	Carta Militar 1:50,000 sheet 10-III, 1:25,000 sheet 114
Refreshments	Café in Soutelo
Access	On the A4 west of Vila Real, take exit 22 (M1240). Follow this south for about 5km to the start.
Parking	Car park next to the chapel

This is a there-and-back hike – only intermittently waymarked – to the highest peak in the region: Serra do Marão (1415m). Alvão Nature Park is more strictly called Alvão/Marão, as the two *serras* (mountain ranges) are linked. This peak is close to but not officially in the nature park.

The views are what make this an excellent walk, so don't bother in poor visibility as the plethora of radio masts at the summit are not attractive in themselves. However, they are not visible while you enjoy the stupendous views.

Facing the chapel, turn right and go north on the M1240 road (no name). Ignore the old signs for PR Trilho Senhora da Serra, which is impassable. Take the first left on a cobbled road heading upwards with a small shrine at the corner (again no name to the road). The cobbled road turns into stone path after 400 metres, then after passing the last building the stone path becomes a cart track. Take an acute left uphill on cart track with indistinct signposting.

At a crossroads with a white **water pumping building** on the far left, turn right. This path is relatively flat initially

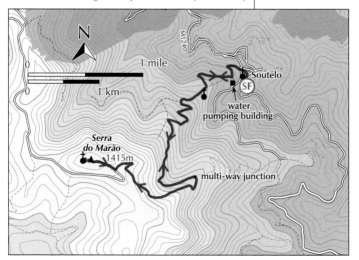

107

Crucifix at the top of Marão with a wind farm in the background

The highest pilgrimage in Portugal is held here on the second Sunday in July and attracts a huge number of people.

but becomes much steeper; it leads to a junction where there is a little chapel ahead. Here the path merges with another path coming uphill; continue right and uphill towards the **chapel**.

After passing the chapel, continue for 400 metres (ignoring a logging path to the right on the way) and then take the first left fork. Follow the main path zigzagging upwards, and whenever there's a choice of route, go upwards. After a steep ascent the route levels and then loops slightly downhill until it reaches a **multi-way junction** of cart tracks just under 3km from the chapel. Turn right here, signposted 'Senhora da Serra 2.3km'.

The cart track becomes a tarmac road and then reverts to a cart track again. About 1.5km from the multi-way junction, arrive at another tarmac road near the summit, where huge numbers of radio masts are visible. Turn right at this junction and aim towards the summit of **Serra do Marão**; there's a massive trig point (a gigantic concrete monolith), a cross, and the Senhora da Serra chapel. ◄

Now retrace steps to Soutelo, enjoying the view of Vila Real to the north-east and Our Lady of Grace in Mondim de Basto (Walk 13) to the north-west. Beware of the tricky turning at the **multi-way junction**: take the first left here, going uphill, signposted 'Soutelo 4km'.

DOURO INTERNATIONAL NATURE PARK

UNESCO-listed terracing along the banks of Rio Douro with wild lavender

Douro is UNESCO World Heritage listed for its cultural landscape and has been a traditional European wine-producing region for over 2000 years. The breathtaking canyon carved by the Rio Douro gives rise to the Mirandese Plateau, interspersed with quartzite ridges, rolling hills, vineyards and olive groves in terraces along the banks of the river. Also worth seeing is the second UNESCO-listed interest in the area: the Paleolithic rock art site on the banks of the Rio Côa, a tributary of the Rio Douro.

The climate has wide temperature ranges with cold winters and very hot, dry summers. Almond blossom, broom, rock rose and lavender are in full bloom in spring, complementing the beautiful scenery. The autumnal colours of deciduous trees and vines provide a contrasting picture; a golden and resplendent landscape. Many species of bird live and breed in the rocky granite cliffs of the canyon, including Egyptian vultures, golden eagles, griffon vultures and black stork.

Road signs in the area feature both Portuguese and Mirandese, the second official language of Portugal. (Mirandese is a Romance language that shares some vocabulary with Portuguese but is more closely related to Spanish. It is spoken by about 15,000 people and only in north-east Portugal.)

BASES

Both Vila Nova de Foz Côa and Mogadouro cater for tourists, and they are about an hour from the start of the walks.

WALK 15
Azeite, Bruçó

Start/Finish	End of Rua Da Praça, Bruçó (N41°14.416′ W06°40.659′)
Distance	8.5km
Total ascent	440m
Grade	Easy
Time	3½hrs
Terrain	All offroad, on a mixture of cobbled and dirt farm tracks
Map	Carta Militar 1:50,000 sheet 11-II, 1:25,000 sheet 120
Refreshments	Bar/café on Rua das Flores; drinking water in town square (Largo da Calçada in Bruçó)
Access	From Mogadouro, take N221 south. Then take M596, followed by N596-1 to Bruçó. Head south from the town square, then the first left heading east.
Parking	At start. (If full of farm machinery, park in town.)
Note	Given the lack of shade on the route, it's best to either start very early or reserve it for a cooler day.

This is based on the official Azeite – 'olive oil' – route, part of which is now impassable. Starting in a quiet stone-built town, it's a there-and-back walk that passes formidable cliffs and goes through ancient terraced olive groves that are still in use. The narrowness of these schist-built terraces means that all the agricultural work, including harvesting, is still done by hand. The route eventually arrives at the water's edge, a restful place to admire the calm waters of Rio Douro and excellent views of the valley. The shade here is also particularly welcome.

Look out for Egyptian vultures and royal eagles (the Portuguese name for golden eagles) while you walk.

The walk starts at a noticeboard at the end of Rua Da Praça. From here, the dirt track immediately forks; go left. Shortly afterwards go past a **large water trough** and a square white building adjacent to a tiny round building. Take the next right-hand fork and after 200 metres arrive at a large stone-built, tile-roofed tractor shed. Continue east along a cobbled road.

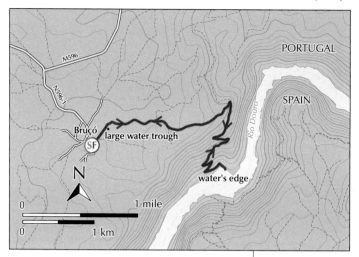

The path becomes cobbled interspersed with sections of dirt road; continue straight on, ignoring the few turnings. The path winds its way downwards through olive groves, heading towards the gargantuan valley.

After about 20mins the route becomes fully cobbled and zigzags steeply into the valley, then zigzags for about 30mins to the **water's edge**, where there's a building surrounded by a solid-looking fence.

The tranquil green waters of Rio Douro

111

There's a path going behind the building where there's a table. Officially this is a boat stop, although there's no pier. Despite the attractive green cool **water** there is no easy place to enter for a swim, but it's a good spot for admiring the scenery, watching the occasional gentle splash from fish, listening to the soothing hum of insects in the distance and the melodious chirp of cicada.

Follow the route back to the start, bearing in mind that the ascent will take longer, and the timing will also depend on the heat.

WALK 16

Ribeira do Mosteiro

Start/Finish	Small car park on N221 (N41°02.272′ W06°54.463′)
Distance	9km
Total ascent	380m
Grade	Easy
Time	3½hrs
Terrain	A mixture of cart tracks, two *calçadas* (sections of ancient stone pavement), footpaths and paved road
Map	Carta Militar 1:50,000 sheet 15-I, 1:25,000 sheet 142
Access	On the N221 from Barca d'Alva towards Freixo de Espada à Cinta, the start is 3.3km after the bridge over Rio Douro.
Parking	At start

The Ribeira do Mosteiro ('river of the monastery') walk may be short but it's a real joy, especially in spring when you'll be walking through a verdant landscape surrounded by a plethora of wildflowers in a riot of colours, bathed in their delicate scents. There is also the possibility of exploring the inside of a *pombal* (pigeon house) and some medieval stone graves, as well as the certainty of seeing griffon vultures and walking on not just one but two different ancient *calçadas*.

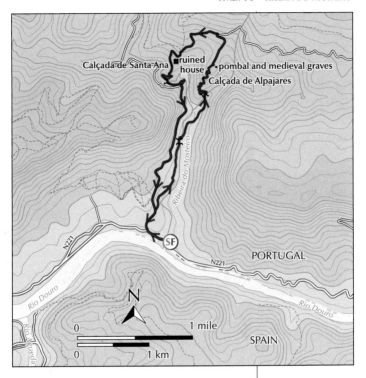

From the start, head west for 250 metres along the N221. Turn right up a roughly tarmacked track, following red/yellow waymarking and signs for Ribeiro do Mosteiro. After 350 metres take a turning on the right to a cart track. Continue for 1km and cross over the river via a **concrete bridge**, then immediately turn left along a footpath heading upstream, signposted Alpajares. This meets a cart track after 250 metres; head left, and then take the signposted footpath on the right (the cart track turns left and goes downhill), still heading upstream.

This lovely footpath soon crosses over a tributary of the river via a small wooden **bridge**. It then zigzags up for about 1km on the ancient stone-built **Calçada**

113

de Alpajares. At the top, the route becomes a cart track heading slightly downhill.

> Just off the path to the right there is a restored ***pombal***, which welcomes visitors, and two medieval graves carved into the rock below some ancient terracing. Portugal is one of the few places to see pigeon houses; found north of Rio Tejo, and are usually round or horseshoe-shaped with either flat or pointed roofs. They were once widely used, the young birds being a source of food and the droppings high-quality fertilizer.

The route becomes tarmacked. About 500 metres from the *pombal*, turn left, signposted for Calçada de Santa Ana (just after a hairpin bend to the right). The path immediately splits into two; take the left lower one. At a crossroads 700 metres later, turn left and go downhill.

Continue, ignoring a right-hand turn, to go past a large **ruined house** on the left after 130 metres, and then zigzag down the ***calçada*** to a bridge. Ascend another *calçada* for 400 metres to its top, pass a shrine and arrive at a roughly paved road. Turn left, downhill. ◀ Follow this for about 2.5km back to the **N221** and turn left to get back to the start.

There are views of impressive red crags on the right.

Calçada de Santa Ana with interesting geology (folds and vertical layers of quartzites) in the background

CENTRAL PORTUGAL
AND LISBON

Hiking along the GR29 through golden grasses with extensive vistas (Walk 30)

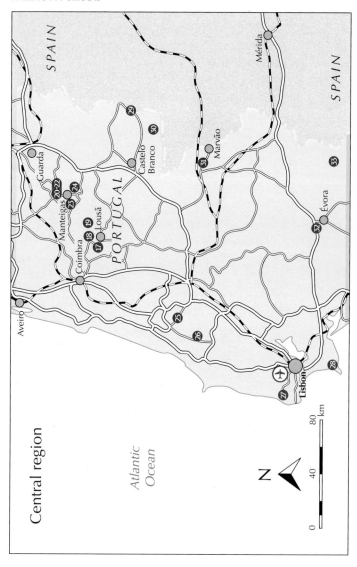

SCHIST VILLAGES

Lagar da Cabreira (Walk 19)

Schist is a type of crystalline metamorphic stone that is easily split to provide an ideal flat building material, and is abundant in this region of Central Portugal. It is used to construct houses and for paving the narrow higgledy-piggledy winding alleyways in the so-called 'schist villages' (*aldeais do xisto*). These villages occupy the highest topographical positions as historical defensive bastions and strategic points of trade routes, looking like rock formations as they nestle in an incredible landscape that includes the Serra da Lousã and Açor mountain ranges.

Hundreds of years ago (and right up until recent decades) the locals walked or travelled by mule along these ancient paths as their only means of communication between villages. During the politically unsettled times and economic depression of the Salazar dictatorship, many villages were deserted as the locals emigrated to various different countries. These splendid villages are now being restored to their former glory using traditional techniques.

BASES

Lousã (the start for Walk 17) is the largest town in the area with all the usual facilities. It is a good base from which to explore the region, and is less than an hour from Walks 18 and 19. It is possible to stay in the remote villages of Talasnal and Candal (on Walk 17) in order to appreciate their location, culture, traditional agricultural practice and history.

WALK 17
Schist villages of Lousã

Start/Finish	Companhia do Papel do Prado (paper mill), Lousã (N40°06.135′ W08°14.728′)
Distance	18.5km
Total ascent	1400m
Grade	Challenging
Time	9hrs
Terrain	All footpaths, some very rough and difficult to walk
Map	Carta Militar 1:50,000 sheet 19-II, 1:25,000 sheet 252
Refreshments	Cafés in Candal and below the castle at Lousã
Toilets	Santuário Nossa Senhora da Piedade
Access	From Lousã train station, head south on Rua Coimbra which becomes Rua Dr Francisco Viana, leading to the start (2km). The paper mill is at the south end of Rua Dr António Lemos.
Parking	At start
Note	GPS recommended
Warning	Stream crossings may be difficult after heavy rain

This superb lengthy walk is a challenge, but it's more than worth the effort. After inauspicious beginnings the route follows some of the most beautiful forest paths in Portugal – the only means for locals traveling between the villages until recent years. Highlights include the schist villages themselves, a sanctuary, a castle, a *levada* (water channel), a still-operational hydroelectric station, and multiple ruined watermills. In almost continuous shade, this walk could even be done in high summer (although note the significant ascent).

The walk amalgamates the official PR 1, 2, 3, 4 and 5 routes, containing some challenging sections both in terms of navigation (hence GPS is especially useful) and terrain, and will leave you feeling that you've really accomplished something.

Note that the time given above is pure walking time, not including time for exploration of the highlights. To shorten the walk you could follow PR5 from Talasnal to the *levada*, leading to the hydroelectric power station (this is not described here; 8.5km, 740m ascent, allow 4½hrs). Alternatively you could split the route into a multiday walk by staying in the schist villages.

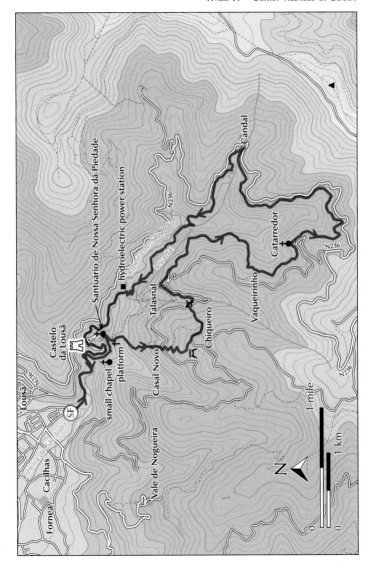

119

Just before the gate of the paper mill, turn left onto the dirt road signposted PR1 (waymarked red/yellow) and walk along this acacia tree-lined path adjacent to a *levada* in the shade. Shortly after crossing a bridge over the *levada*, take the right-hand path across the stream and head uphill (to the left is the return route).

Zigzag uphill for 200 metres, with the sound of the river flowing beneath and views of the castle on the other side of the valley. Continue straight ahead at a junction, leading to a **small chapel** with a *cruzeiro* (cross) monument at the top of a mound.

Exit on the other side of the mound and turn right, heading south-east, soon with a view of the ethereal Santuário de Nossa Senhora da Piedade. Ford a small stream and head up a steep staircase to reach a folly-like structure with a terrace upstairs and a shelter downstairs with windows and picnic tables. Continue along the path and take the first right fork. There are a few paths along the way leading to various terraces; continue for 250 metres to the **sanctuary**.

The **Sanctuary of Our Lady of Pity** is a complex of four chapels. Saint John's is the largest and the oldest,

Santuário de Nossa Senhora da Piedade and Castelo da Lousã in the verdant landscape

dating from the 15th century, whereas the white-painted Chapel of Our Lady was probably built in the 17th century, famed for its limestone sculpture which is brought out once a year for a procession. The Chapel of the Lord of Agony dates from the 18th century, and the most recent is the Chapel of the Lord of the Afflicted (1912), noted for its sculptures.

Immediately take the stairs on the right, now following blue/yellow waymarking with signs for Casal Novo, Talasnal, and Chiqueiro. About 200 metres up, take a small turning on the right leading to a **platform** with a cross and good views and seating. Behind the cross, take the steep stairs uphill (on first entering the platform the stairs are on the left. Ignore the steps across the platform going down, waymarked yellow/red). At the top of the steep stairs is a footpath leading to multiple paths; take the first right, signposted PR5 to Casal Novo, heading south. ▶ This is a very steep path, which after a long ascent crosses a cart track and then continues further uphill.

All these paths are red/yellow waymarked PR routes; be sure to follow the correct one.

About 700 metres from the signpost, arrive at **Casal Novo** and turn left just before the first building to enter the village. At the next T-junction, with a well-built stone footpath, turn right, walking between buildings. This leads to the outskirts of the village, where there is a paved area with good views of Lousã.

Take the first left (before exiting the village), leading back into the middle of the village (don't follow the sign for PR2). Just before exiting the village to the south, take a right turn, uphill, following signs for PR5 to Chiqueiro (not to the castle).

Walk up the steep steps to a road, and turn right. After 30 metres turn left into a cart track signposted PR5 to Chiqueiro. Follow this upwards for 700 metres, arrive at a road and turn left, downhill. ▶

There's a picnic area to the right and uphill.

Walk through the village of **Chiqueiro**. There's a sign for PR5 on entry to the village, pointing downhill and down the steps (but after that no more signs). Walk down the steps, and at the bottom of the village turn right and curve leftwards until the path has reversed its direction.

Then walk along a wall, through a terraced area below the village, leading to a bulldozed cart track. Go across, almost straight ahead (slightly to the right), taking a narrow unsigned footpath heading steeply downhill among pine trees.

This leads to a road after 250 metres; turn right and then almost immediately take the downhill unsigned footpath on the left (just before the crash barrier starts). Continue on this path for 700 metres, crossing over a grassy **bridge** to reach **Talasnal**.

Walk along the very narrow, one-person-wide stone-built street and arrive at multiple paths. Follow PR4 signed for Vaqueirinho, zigzagging up the ramp to the village fountain, where there's a square with signs for various houses and a restaurant. Cross this square to the tarmac road, walk uphill for about 200 metres and take the wide footpath on the left just off the corner of the hairpin bend. After passing another bend, take a narrow waymarked footpath forking right uphill, winding its way through deciduous forest. ◄

After 800 metres reach a slippery section with steel cables for assistance, and then continue on this route to the remains of ancient terracing. Walk between two drystone walls, and then fork left. The path zigzags for 150 metres up to **Vaqueirinho**. Take the main steps to the left, curve left then go uphill. This is a bit of a maze, with steps leading everywhere, so if in doubt, just aim upwards until you arrive at a more open space with a *lavadouro* (communal clothes-washing place) and an amazing agave plant.

Exit the village via a path near the *lavadouro* at the upper left corner of the square, on a stone-built ramp leading to a T-junction with a dirt track. Turn left, signposted PR4 to Catarredor. After 50 metres the track curves left; take a signposted footpath on the right. Follow this beautiful and easy-to-follow footpath for 800 metres to **Catarredor**.

In the village the path curves up. Walk through the village, not taking any small paths off the main street, then reach a waymarked set of steps heading upwards

Lousã, the highest peak in the range, is visible to the east (see Walk 18).

on the right. This leads to a **chapel** and tarmac road at the top of the village. (Another maze of streets; if lost, head to the highest point of the village.)

Walk along the tarmac road, up and out of the village. At the hairpin bend, take the footpath leaving the road on the left, signposted PR4 to Candal. After 1km, take an easily missed small downhill footpath forking off to the left just after a bend at a stream (the main well-travelled path leads to mountain bike route XC12).

Continue on a steep, stony and narrow descent, followed immediately by a similar ascent. There's a lot of up and down, and it's a narrow, difficult-to-walk path with some scrambling, but it's well waymarked. This section is just over 2km.

Arrive at a wide cart track with a fork, and go left and downhill. The cart track then becomes a footpath again, heading east. This leads to a junction, where PR3 and PR4 intersect. Turn acutely left, doubling back and heading downhill towards the river. Pass some ruined schist houses of old **Candal**, then turn right to cross the foot bridge. Follow the track between more ruined schist buildings. ▶

There are cafés on the main road in Candal if you fancy a bite to eat.

Halfway up this track towards a road, take the left-hand fork, heading downhill. Turn right after 150 metres,

The schist village of Candal nestled beneath Serra da Lousã

signed 'Central' ('Cascata' is to the left), and go up a narrow stony path, leading to an easy footpath.

After 500m go straight over a cart track and continue for 200m before the footpath starts to go downhill. The route then starts zigzag down steeply after 200m, it is quite easy to follow but not easy to walk.

It reaches a **levada**; turn left and walk along the *levada* which then curves to the right and crosses over a bridge. Continue following the *levada* downstream with some significant drops on the right. ◄

Reach the end of the 1.5km-long *levada* at a junction of PR3 merging with PR5 and continue to follow PR3 downhill towards Castelo, along a large water pipe then across a bridge to the **hydroelectric power station**.

This was the first **hydroelectric power station** ever built in Portugal. It was constructed in 1927 and is still in use today. In 2017, hydroelectric power accounts for more than 37% of the total energy production in Portugal. The country's eventual aim is to use 100% renewable power.

In some sections there are barriers/handrails but others are more intimidating.

The levada leading to the hydroelectric plant

Walk past the station then along the dirt track uphill, and follow the dirt track towards the castle. Arrive at tarmac road after just over 1km and turn left (downhill) to the front of the **castle**, then walk along the cobbled path to the left-hand side of the castle, waymarked yellow/red (a swimming area and restaurant are at the end of the tarmac road).

> **Castelo da Lousã**, also known as Castelo de Arouce, once defended the routes to Coimbra. Occupied by the Moors in 1124, it was retaken, earning itself a Royal Charter in 1151.

Continue for 150 metres to a building with a disused toilet and take the path to the left of it. Go under the cable (which supplies the sanctuary shelter), then zigzag steeply downhill towards the river. Pass the first ruined watermill and cross the river via stepping-stones. Follow the footpath on the true left side of the river, walking a short distance before re-crossing the river (with a second watermill). Continue to cross and re-cross the river several times, with some more mills. On the final occasion, crossing this time from true left to the other side, arrive at the *levada* that was encountered at the beginning of the walk. Retrace steps to the start in **Lousã**.

WALK 18

*Caminho do Xisto das Aldeias de
Góis and Lousã summit*

Start/Finish	Comareira (N40°07.610′ W08°09.214′)
Distance	8.5km; including Lousã summit: 16km
Total ascent	550m; including Lousã summit: 950m
Grade	Medium; including Lousã summit: difficult
Time	3½hrs; including Lousã summit: 6½hrs
Terrain	PR1 is mainly on good footpaths; the route to the summit is on cart track
Map	Carta Militar 1:50,000 sheet 19-II, 1:25,000 sheets 242 and 252
Refreshments	Café in Aigra Nova; seasonal mobile café near Lousã summit
Access	Approximately 10.5km from Lousã towards Góis on the N342, take the small road on the right, signposted Comareira.
Parking	There are four parking spaces on the left as you enter the hamlet.

The official PR1 Caminho do Xisto das Aldeias de Góis ('route of the ancient schist villages of Góis') is a lovely little circular route taking you through four traditional schist villages, woodlands and moors. An ascent of the highest peak in the mountain range, Lousã (1205m; also known as Castelo do Trevim), is included here as an optional extra. Although not especially pretty in itself, it does give the best views in the area.

The official walk begins in Aigra Nova but parking there is more difficult so the route described here starts slightly lower down. It is waymarked yellow/red except for the path to the summit.

From the parking area, walk uphill along the tarmac road towards Aigra Nova, following PR1. After 400 metres fork right, down to a cart track, looking out in the distance for the optional summit of Lousã with its radio masts.

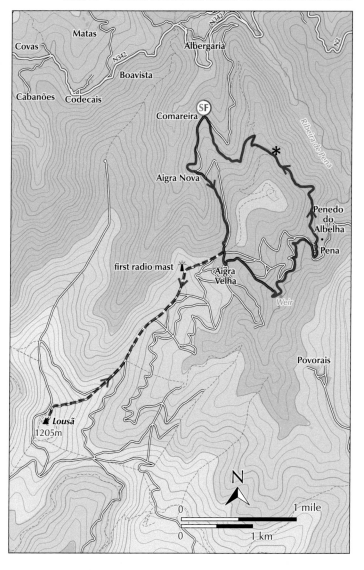

View back to Aigra Nova

When the cart track becomes a cobbled road after 500 metres you've reached the village of **Aigra Nova**. ◀ Follow the cobbled road and arrive at the town square (Largo da Quinta); go straight ahead and walk past a water tap, along Rua dos Sobreiros (go left to visit the museum and café). Arrive at a three-way junction and take the footpath in the middle, heading south-east (ignore the tarmac road to the left and a grassy path to the right). Continue along this easy-to-follow footpath with no turnings, leading to a tarmac road. Turn right and go uphill on the tarmac road for 80 metres to reach its crest.

There is a café in the village.

To climb the Lousã summit

At the crest of the road, with a signpost on the left for Pena, take the unsigned dirt track on the right. Continue on the dirt track, ignoring turnings, and walk past the first **radio mast**. At the first fork go right and uphill, heading towards the summit. Ignore a turning on the left and arrive at a crossroads 1.5km after the radio mast; go right (south-west). Ignore another left-hand turn 500 metres further on, and 70 metres later go left at a fork (the summit is just ahead but obscured by pine trees) along a lesser-travelled track.

Reach a T-junction after 700 metres, turn left, and 100 metres later arrive at the summit of **Lousã**, which in typical Portuguese fashion is festooned with radio masts, a variety of buildings and a huge trig point. Retrace the route from the summit back to the tarmac road and turn right towards Aigra Velha.

Walk down the tarmac road and arrive at **Aigra Velha**, where the road changes to cobbles. The route turns acutely left before entering the village, signed PR1 to Pena.

> **Aigra Velha** is the highest schist village at an altitude of 770m; from it you can see Serra da Estrela (the highest mountain range in mainland Portugal). The 'old' village has its own unique defensive system, created in medieval times, against the weather, intruders and wild animals (especially wolves): they joined their houses together so they didn't need to go outside at night.

The conjoined houses of Aigra Velha

Reach a fork and go right (downhill) on a cart track. About 700 metres later this turns left and almost immediately arrives at a T-junction. Turn right, zigzag downhill, and then take a footpath on the left just before the stream (there's a modern stone house across the water).

The path very soon leads to a stone-built footpath with a **weir** to the right; go downstream and follow this to a cart track. Go straight across and then cross another cart track, staying on the footpath straight ahead. Just over 1km from the weir, arrive at a dirt road and turn right into the village of **Pena**, where underfoot is now a cobbled road.

To the east are Ribeira da Pena and Penedo do Albelha – the massive 'rock of the bees' which is a famous site for climbing.

Walk along Rua da Ponte to the end of the village. Just before the bridge, turn left along a cobbled road going uphill for 150 metres (do not cross the bridge; that is PR9). At the next T-junction turn right and uphill, then go right at the next fork, continuing uphill on Rua do Pelombe, and leave the village on a cobbled road which becomes a dirt track. ◄

The dirt track curves left, heading north-west and leading to a cart track about 400 metres from the village. Go left and uphill for about 10 steps, and then take the footpath going right and downhill. Follow this footpath for just over 1km to the top of a steep hill, which has a crossroads with a **viewpoint** to the right from which the mountain ranges of Serra da Estrela, Serra do Açor and Serra do Lousã are all visible.

After the viewpoint, go straight ahead and then the footpath metamorphoses into a cart track. Take the next right fork and go downhill. After 400 metres, take a left-hand downhill turning. About 500 metres later, take an easily missed right-hand footpath forking off, going downhill through a eucalyptus plantation. Follow it and then cross a cart track to continue on footpath for another 200 metres.

Arrive at another cart track and follow it leftwards. When the cart track becomes a footpath, take a difficult-to-see but signed left uphill fork. Reach a tarmac road, turn left uphill and return to the start at **Comareira**.

WALK 19

Trilho do Vale do Ceira,
Cabreira

Start/Finish	Lagar da Cabreira (old olive mill), Cabreira (N40°08.508′ W08°04.014′)
Distance	13km
Total ascent	800m
Grade	Medium
Time	5½hrs
Terrain	Mostly footpaths, some dirt tracks, almost all off-road. Some of the paths are very narrow with precipitous drops.
Map	Carta Militar 1:50,000 sheet 20-III, 1:25,000 sheet 243
Refreshments	Café in Cabreira
Toilets	In Cadafaz (also at start but might be locked)
Access	Go east from the village of Cabreira on the M543 towards Sandinha. The start is about 500 metres on the right after exiting the village.
Parking	On left-hand side of road opposite Lagar da Cabreira
Note	GPS recommended

The length and ascent involved in PR3 Trilho do Vale do Ceira ('path of the valley of Ceira') may not sound like much but it's quite a tough walk, undulating significantly with no flat easy sections at all. The scenery along the Rio Ceira valley is quite beautiful, with a deserted schist village, two inhabited ones, and plenty of waterfalls.

The route is signposted but waymarking might be missing, due to tree logging or eucalyptus shedding its bark, making navigation difficult sometimes.

In season you can eat wild fruits along the way on deserted terraced orchards and see plants uncommon in the rest of Portugal: rose of Sharon and hellebores. There are scattered ruinous schist buildings among semi-shaded woodland full of laurel, oak, elm, elder, arbutus, olive and birch. The route has enough shade for summer walking, with the added bonus of a place for a swim at the end.

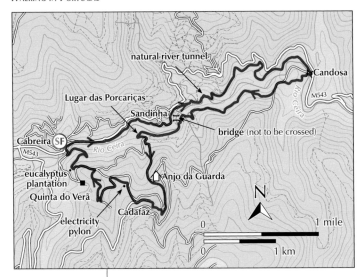

From the car parking area, cross the road and walk down the cobbles to the deserted schist-built complex, where there's a noticeboard for PR3.

> The water-powered **olive oil mill and press** have been here for over a century; they are still operational and used for ad hoc demonstrations. The olives of 11 local villages used to be transported here by river before being pressed to produce olive oil.

Follow the yellow/red waymarking towards the buildings, away from the bridge. There is a shaded picnic area. (Be careful not to follow signs for PR6 close to the start.) Go upstream along the beautiful tree-lined river, past the buildings on the left, and then take a steeply ascending footpath on the left to the road. Turn right and walk along it for about 200 metres, then take a footpath on the right next to the telegraph pole, going downhill initially then gently upwards.

Walk along the disused ancient terracing and go gently uphill. ▶ The surroundings gradually become actively cultivated, leading to the village of **Sandinha** after walking 1km on this footpath. At the first house/building take the right fork and go slightly downhill. Go through the outskirts of the village along this cart track, now going uphill. When the cart track turns acutely left towards the road, take the footpath on the right off this bend heading north-east, going downhill. Reach another cart track after 100 metres, turn left and immediately right, crossing over the cart track. (This footpath is not well-trodden or marked.)

Go straight ahead at a crossroads after just under 200 metres; the path then curves left and downhill. Continue walking along a section with a big drop and the river on the right, and soon come to a **natural river tunnel** with two schist houses above it. Arrive at a junction and go left (right goes to the two schist houses with views down the river). On the other side of the river tunnel, reach a cart track and go uphill. Continue until the main cart track turns acutely left and slightly uphill; turn right here onto a less-travelled cart track, going slightly downhill. This then becomes a narrow footpath.

Grapes, figs, olives, apples, peaches and rosemary are still growing, indicating that this used to be arable land.

Two ruined schist houses above the natural river tunnel

The path becomes a cart track 400 metres later. When this turns acutely left uphill, take the footpath straight ahead and downwards, towards a building. This leads to a crossroads with a disused cart track; go straight across. Arrive at a fork after 200 metres and take the smaller, lower right-hand branch. Shortly after, there's a view of the valley with a river, a wooden bridge and the village of Candosa on the right.

Go right and downhill at the first fork, then go left and uphill at the second fork (otherwise the path will lead to the wooden bridge). When the footpath gets to two small buildings, turn off to the smaller, lower right-hand track with a road bridge visible ahead. After 300 metres reach the tarmac road, turn right and cross the **bridge**, then turn left immediately after the bridge to enter **Candosa**, with a shaded picnic area on the left.

At a T-junction in the village, turn left. The path curves right and uphill, and then goes over a little *levada* (water channel) with views of waterfalls and a watermill. Follow the main path to a tarmac road, turn left and uphill, then 150 metres later take the first right-hand dirt road.

Sea of mountains in Serra da Lousã

Approximately 1.5km after leaving the tarmac road, follow red/yellow waymarking to turn right onto an indistinct small footpath, at a point where the two previous schist houses above the river tunnel are visible on the opposite side of the valley (if this turning is missed, there's a 90° left-hand bend on the dirt road later; retrace steps from there).

The footpath meets a bulldozed path; go straight across and continue for about 150 metres. Next cross a little bridge with old disused terracing nearby, then go down a set of steps and reach a bridge over Rio Ceira. Do not cross this bridge; stay on this side of the river. Continue to follow the river downstream for 500 metres to a fork, where cultivated terraces and a white-painted clocktower are visible across the other side of the valley. Here go left and uphill, leading after 150 metres to a disused building which is almost all that is left of the abandoned village of **Lugar das Porcariças**. Turn left and uphill just after it on a cart track which then crosses a dirt road.

> **Lugar das Porcariças** (meaning 'place of the pig-keepers') was inhabited from Roman times, and formerly had a population of 150. Damaged extensively by severe thunderstorms in 1896 and 1939, it never completely recovered and was eventually abandoned.

The path becomes an overgrown cart track and zig-zags steeply uphill. At the first fork, go left and uphill, shortly after which there's another fork. Go right (this is less steep than the left-hand option), then soon after at another fork take the left-hand uphill option. ▶

Continue for 300 metres to reach a dirt road with the village of Cadafaz visible on the right, across the valley. Turn right onto this dirt road, and 100 metres later take a little footpath on the left heading steeply upwards next to a wall. Follow it towards the village for a short distance, then take a path forking off to the right, smaller and more level. Follow this as it curves around the valley, then take

Just after these forks there's a shelter with a ceramic-tiled plaque dedicated to Anjo da Guarda (guardian angels).

a set of stairs going up through a gap in the wall on the left, leading immediately to **Cadafaz**.

In the village, turn right and follow the path which becomes a cobbled narrow road next to the Casa Mortuaria (mortuary). ◀ Pass the mortuary and walk to the end of the church. Turn right (not going up the steps; the waymarking is confusing here) and continue along the cobbled street, which is called Rua Doctor Oliveira Salazar.

Go past a little chapel on the right, then 200 metres later take the first cart track on the right. This is cobbled initially with a shrine from 1964 on its left. Arrive at an **electricity pylon**, where there are two left-hand turnings; take the second one, which goes underneath the power cables heading north. This is immediately followed by a fork; take the right-hand, more level branch.

This leads to a dirt road, where you turn left. Continue along this dirt road for about 450 metres to arrive at a T-junction with another dirt road. Turn right and go downhill. Zigzag down to a house and take a footpath on the right, going behind it and heading north. Walk past some cultivated land to a T-junction with another dirt track and turn right, heading north-east. Ignore a turning to the right and continue for 70 metres from the T-junction to a crossroads with a dirt track. Go left and downhill, heading west.

About 450 metres after the crossroads, after passing under a telegraph cable, at a **eucalyptus plantation** take a logging track to the right and downhill, with a view of Cabreira (if this turning is missed, the dirt track would arrive at Quinta do Verã). Follow the logging track to leave the eucalyptus plantation behind and enter deciduous woodland.

When the cart track starts to go uphill, take a left-hand track nearly doubling back. This dirt track becomes a footpath, leading to a T-junction with a cart track 400 metres after the last turn. Go right and downhill, being careful not to follow PR6 waymarking. This leads to the bridge; cross it and return to the start at **Cabreira**, where you may be tempted to take a dip in the river.

There are toilets here.

SERRA DA ESTRELA NATURE PARK

Panoramic view of Manteigas with an autumnal foreground of Pyrenean oak (Walk 21)

The 'Star' mountain range has an alpine, mountainous landscape strongly influenced by glaciation, creating an interesting morphology with boulders, moraines, glacial lagoons and deep U–shaped valleys. The area is dominated by granitic rocks of over 300 million years old. Torre (Walk 23) is the highest point in mainland Portugal at 1993m (2000m if you include the stone monument built at the top by Dom João VI).

Visit between December and May to admire the snow-capped mountains, or September and October for autumnal colours. May and June, however, are perhaps the best months to visit, in order to appreciate the alpine wildflowers. Summer tends to be very busy.

There are only four villages above 900m: Manteigas, Sabugueiro, Penhas da Saúde and Folgosinho. The latter is the most picturesque. A visit to the villages is recommended whether you're staying in them or not, in order to appreciate the culture and traditions adapted to the environment, and to taste the local cuisine: Estrela cheese and suckling pig. The Estrela mountain dogs (*Cão da Serra da Estrela*) – massive, loyal creatures with fuzzy golden and black puppies – will win anybody over.

BASES

Manteigas (the start point for Walks 20, 21 and 22, and the finish point for Walk 23) is the best base from which to explore the area with ample accommodation, restaurants and shops. Walk 24 is a short distance away by car.

WALK 20
Sol and Rota das Faias, Manteigas

Start/Finish	Tourist office in Manteigas (N40°24.173′ W07°32.200′)
Distance	11km
Total ascent	600m
Grade	Medium
Time	4½hrs
Terrain	Mostly on good footpaths
Map	Adventure Maps Serra da Estrela; Carta Militar 1:50,000 sheet 17-II, 1:25,000 sheet 213
Refreshments	In Manteigas
Toilets	In Manteigas

This route, named 'sun and beech' in this guide, combines the official PR11 Sol ('sun') and PR13 Rota das Faias ('route of the beeches'), so that the walk starts from Manteigas town with no need to drive. It doesn't go massively high (the highest point is the Chapel of St Lawrence, which is above the trig point of São Lourenço at 1176m), yet it has some excellent views and the section on soft paths shaded by beeches is a delight. This is an ideal walk when the summits are shrouded in mists, or in the summer as shade is frequent.

From the tourist office, walk across the road and up the tarmac road, following signs for Gouveia. Take the first turning on the right – Rua Quinta de São Fernando, a small tarmac road heading downhill, waymarked PR11 (opposite a cobbled road on the left). Walk past the **Fonte dos Namorados**, which means 'fountain of the boyfriends/sweethearts'.

Reach a T-junction with another cobbled road about 1km from the fountain and turn left uphill, following PR13. ◀

Be careful to follow the correct waymarking as PR11 and PR13 intersect here.

On arrival at a fork after 200 metres, go right: this becomes a dirt road. Continue along the very pretty valley full of vines and smallholdings. After 500 metres, cross over a **bridge** and then after a steep ascent reach a crossroads with another dirt track and turn left, following

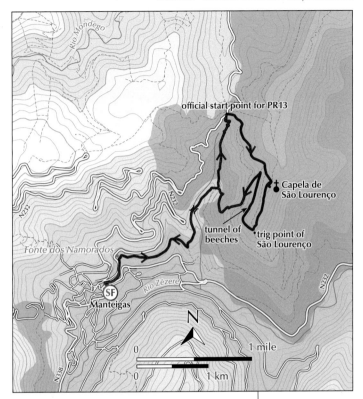

PR13 (straight ahead is the return route). When the dirt road becomes a footpath, look behind for some impressive views of Manteigas and the Zêzere valley. Walk up this steep, good-quality footpath to a tarmac road (1km from the crossroads), which is the **official start point for PR13**.

Turn right and walk east along a dirt road (be careful as PR14 and PR15 are also around here) and then take the first fork to the left uphill on a rough cart track. Ignore a turning to the right next to a ruined house, then go left at a fork (uphill). After 250 metres, at the top of that gentle rise, reach a T-junction with another dirt road and turn right. Immediately after the turn, to the left is the still-used **Capela de São Lourenço** (chapel).

> The **Chapel of St Lawrence** is at the highest point of the walk at 1194m, providing superb views. It has been a place of worship since pre-history, when it was the point at which the summer solstice would be first seen from Manteigas. Appropriately for this walk, worship of trees and the sun also occurred here. According to legend, an image of Saint Lawrence disappeared from the chapel in Sicó and reappeared here, leading to the building of the chapel. It was last reconstructed in the 17th century.

Continue along the dirt road for 500 metres to the **trig point of São Lourenço** with a lookout tower. About 80 metres from the tower, take a signposted faint cart track on the right, heading north-west (ignore some other tracks in both directions) and walk through a resplendent **tunnel of beeches**.

View of southern part of Manteigas

The **beech forest** was planted by Manteigas Forest Service in 1888 to combat severe erosion. This used up grazing land and was so unwelcome to the local shepherds that the army had to be called out to quell their violent protests.

At the bottom of this tunnel, reach a T-junction with another dirt road and turn acutely left and downhill. Arrive at a multi-way junction at a hut with two roads forking ahead; take the right fork, heading downhill. After 300 metres take a faint lovely footpath on the right going downwards through the trees; it is signposted but still easy to miss. Cross over a cart track, take the next left (before the path reaches a house), and then immediately take a footpath downhill on the right.

This leads back, after 80 metres, to the crossroads with the dirt track encountered earlier; go straight ahead, initially on cobbles and then on a dirt road signposted 'Vila de Manteigas'. Retrace steps back to the start in **Manteigas**.

WALK 21
Rota do Carvão, Manteigas

Start/Finish	Câmara Municipal (town hall), Manteigas (N40°24.034′ W07°32.460′)
Distance	21km
Total ascent	1150m
Grade	Challenging
Time	8hrs
Terrain	Excellent footpaths, forest tracks, and cart tracks across a high plateau
Map	Adventure Maps Serra da Estrela; Carta Militar 1:50,000 sheets 17-II and 20-I, 1:25,000 sheets 212, 213, 223 and 224
Refreshments	In Manteigas
Access	The town hall is on Rua 1° de Maio
Parking	Car park opposite town hall or on the road

PR4 Rota do Carvão ('the coal route') is a challenging and rewarding walk across a superb mix of terrains, with a good stiff climb to a high plateau among some of the best landscapes in Portugal. The views on a good day are excellent; you should aim to do this route in clear conditions.

The summit of Curral do Martins (1721m) is added here for its impressive vistas of the whole plateau plus Torre (Walk 23). The route is reasonably well waymarked throughout with only occasionally difficult navigation, but there is no waymarking at all in the town.

> The official name of this walk refers to the historic use of the route; the enterprising locals collected heather roots here, which were then burned to produce **charcoal**.

Facing the town hall, go left and uphill on a cobbled road, at the end of which turn left onto Rua Dr Sobral. Turn right up a set of steps, with a signpost detailing the walk at the bottom. After the steps is a cobbled road; go to its end and turn right, walking past Santa Casa da Misericordia.

Take the first left turn, and then the first right turn onto Rua Joaquim Pereiras de Matos, followed by the first left, which is uphill. Then take the third left-hand road, Rua Dr Afonso Costa, waymarked red/white/yellow (PR4 and 16). Ignore a right-hand turn, then go straight ahead and uphill at a crossroads. Go left at a T-junction, and at the next T-junction 450 metres later, turn left and uphill which is well signposted (the main path goes right and downhill). Take the next right-hand turning, still going uphill on cobbles.

Ignoring any turnings, zigzag up a steep ascent to a tarmac road, and then go right and uphill. The tarmac road very quickly becomes a stone-cobbled uphill path, which then curves to the left. Again ignoring all turnings, pass the old **Casa do Guarda-Florestal da Carvalheira** after 100 metres, and then after a further 700 metres reach a tarmac road and turn right. Some

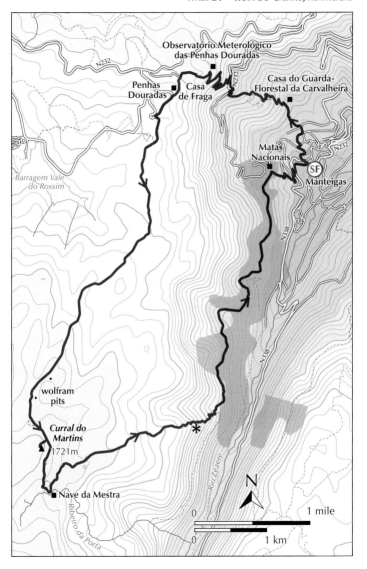

100 metres later arrive at a T-junction with another tarmac road (**N232**) and go across the road onto a dirt track straight ahead, heading north-west. Go past picnic tables and a water tank, and turn right once back on the tarmac road.

After 100 metres take the first left turning; an acutely angled cart track heading upwards just by a 'STOP' sign. Zigzag up to a T-junction with another dirt road and go left along the signposted PR4 Vale das Éguas ('valley of the mares'). ◄ Arrive at a tarmac road after 250 metres with the **Observatório Meterológico das Penhas Douradas** (Golden Rocks Meteorological Observatory) on the right, and go left. After a further 200 metres take an indistinct footpath on the left, waymarked red/white.

Do not follow the waymarking to the right for PR15.1.

Walk through a copse of Douglas firs (rare around here) to arrive at a confusing multi-way junction of very rough cart tracks. Turn left, then fork right immediately, going uphill and due south (if viewed as one big junction then it's the second exit from the left). After 200 metres, arrive at the tarmac road just by **Casa de Fraga**, an impressive stone structure on the right. Turn left, and 400

Casa de Fraga in Penhas Douradas

144

metres later turn left again (the red/white waymarking goes straight ahead). This sparsely built village is Penhas Douradas (Golden Stones).

> In the 1880s royal physician **Dr Sousa Martins** researched the benefit of clean fresh air for the treatment of tuberculosis. Most subjects died except for Alfredo Cesar Henriques, who was the first man treated and cured at Penhas Douradas. Henriques built Casa de Fraga in 1882 at 1475m altitude, starting the first mountain health resort in Portugal – hence the handful of well-built houses.

Stay on the main tarmac road for 1km until it becomes a dirt road. The next section is stunningly beautiful with smooth, rounded boulders scattered across an extensive plateau that seems to extend for miles in all directions – but it does pose navigational difficulties. At a junction where the main dirt road curves right, waymarked in yellow only, go straight ahead waymarked red only, heading towards a dead-end sign and a shack. This is immediately followed by a fork; go right towards the shack (not the dead-end road). Next continue straight ahead on a cart track heading south, ignoring the right-hand path which goes to the shack only.

About 800 metres further on, at a signpost with a fork, go right onto a footpath waymarked red/yellow and marked with cairns (the very rough cart track forks left). This goes past a couple of **wolfram (tungsten ore) pits**. Then ignore a right-hand turn waymarked red only. Caution is required as there are lots of little paths; follow the red/yellow and cairn-waymarked route, aiming towards the summit and its trig point, mostly heading south-west (it's about 4km from the shack to summit).

The summit of **Curral do Martins** is not on the official PR route; to get there, turn right and make your own way for 200 metres to the trig-point-marked summit. Be careful as there's a line of cairns continuing on past the summit which is yet another route. Retrace steps back to the official path.

Once back on the route, continue south. To the left is a cairn-festooned projection of rock which is not the route. After 500m, there are multiple vague paths, bear left (SE) leading to an incredibly narrow gap heading down with steps between two massive boulders known locally as 'the eye of the needle'. It leads directly to **Nave da Mestra**.

> Allow some time to explore the **Nave da Mestra** (Master's Ship). This was a summer holiday house built in 1910, creating a small resort for shepherds and mountaineers. The structure was literally built into the ship-shaped imposing granite boulder, hence the name.

From the house, head north-east through a gap in a wall. (This footpath is very indistinct as it's on bare rock.) Continue walking north-east to a gap in a second wall. The route curves left and then right; ignore a footpath going off to the right. With the trig point on Curral do Martins visible to the north-west, head south-east towards a gap between two stony prominences. About 40 metres before the prominences, turn left (north-east) along a path marked with cairns and very faded red/yellow waymarking. Reach a **viewpoint** just under 2km later.

> The **viewpoint** boasts great views of the Zêrere valley (Walk 23), a huge deep valley sculpted from the granite by a single glacier. Manteigas is visible to the left in the distance.

The path is once again a little indistinct at this point. Zigzag down for 1km to a dirt road and turn left. This is a particularly delightful part of the walk, being gentle and mostly downhill through beautiful woodlands with streams to all sides. Reach a fork just under 2km later and take the left-hand, uppermost option.

After another 2.5km, just before a **Matas Nacionais** building (which is 50 metres from a tarmac road ahead), take the right-hand turn into a cobbled road. This

View of Manteigas from the descent

becomes a grass-covered cart track, heading quite steeply down with a wall on the right-hand side. It leads to a tarmac road after 300 metres; turn right and downhill, past an unusual chapel with a roof like a ski-jump and statue of Mary on top. Continue on the road and curve round the front of the chapel. Take the first right, an acute turn almost doubling back, onto a cobbled road downhill, which becomes a stone road. Just before its end, turn acutely left to arrive at a tarmac road. Turn left and go downhill.

The route curves past another chapel (Capela de São Domingos, built in 1616), and then turns right into a dead-end road, Rua Engenheiro Augusto Barjona de Freitas. Go down the steps on the left before the end of the road. Arrive at another road and turn left towards Colegio Nossa Senhora da Fatima, after which turn right and go down a few steps.

Go left at the next fork after 40 metres, and walk down the steps and cross a bridge. Continue down Rua das Carreiras, a cobbled road between buildings. At its end, turn acutely left just before reaching a church and an exposition hall, almost doubling back to arrive back at the start.

WALK 22

Javali and Poço do Inferno, Manteigas

Start/Finish	Beside Hotel Vale do Zêzere, Manteigas (N40°23.714′ W07°32.235′)
Distance	14km
Total ascent	1100m
Grade	Difficult
Time	6hrs
Terrain	Almost all off-road, some dirt tracks and a lot of forest paths. PR1 has some rock scrambling.
Map	Adventure Maps Serra da Estrela; Carta Militar 1:50,000 sheets 17-II and 20-I, 1:25,000 sheets 213 and 224
Refreshments	In Manteigas
Access	The walk begins from the big sign for PR2 next to the Hotel Vale do Zêzere at the junction of Rua da Lapa and Bairro Campo de Santo António, Manteigas.
Parking	At start

This superb walk combines two already good hikes to make a longer, even more fun and interesting one. There are forest trails, stunning views of mountains, and a photogenic waterfall. PR2 Javali is called the 'wild boar walk', as you can't fail to see evidence of their foraging along the way, with patches of freshly turned soil where they dig for roots and acorns. PR1 Poço do Inferno – 'inferno well' or 'hell's pit' – features a waterfall into a bowl with a 10-metre drop.

With a fair amount of shade this route is suitable for summer walking, but it's at its most attractive in autumn, when the trees become a riot of yellows, browns and oranges.

For a shorter walk it is very easy to do each PR by itself. PR2: 11km, 590m ascent, 4hrs. PR1 (start point N40°22.380′ W07°31.036′): 3km, 200m ascent, 1½hrs.

In addition to the red/ yellow waymarking on this walk, there is also the red/ white of GR33.

From the road junction, walk south-east and uphill. ◄ This becomes a stone road almost immediately. Arrive at a fork after 200 metres, go left, and then turn left at a crossroads with a dirt track signposted PR2 (ahead is the return route).

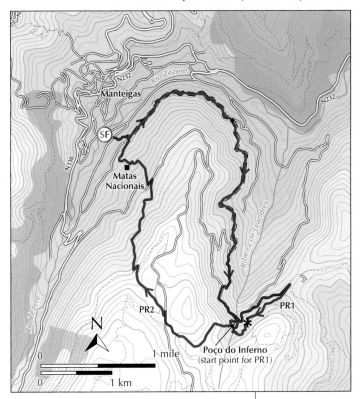

Continue on the dirt track for 1.5km then fork right and uphill (the red/white waymarked GR33 goes left). This leads to another fork after 1.5km; again go right and uphill, then stay on the main path for 750 metres. ▶ Go right and uphill at the next fork, well signposted.

About 200 metres up this dirt track, just when it starts to level off, there's a footpath going off to the right. Follow this narrow footpath, zigzagging steeply up the hill to a tarmac road, and turn left. About 500 metres later arrive at **Poço do Inferno**, with a selection of picnic tables nestled beneath the trees and several viewpoints.

Do not get confused by a red cross which is the mountain bike trail.

149

*The Poço do
Inferno cascade*

Poço do Inferno is a **waterfall** formed by the Ribeira
de Leandres. The water runs over granitic rocks and
then encounters a natural barrier of rocks hardened
by contact metamorphism with pure magma, after
which it plunges 10 metres onto similar but unhard-
ened rocks that have been eroded.

There's a car park just before the waterfalls: routes
PR1 and PR2 both head off on the right-hand side here,
behind a big sign. At a fork 100 metres up this path, go
left to follow PR1 (the right fork is for PR2, to be used
later). Very shortly after this PR1/PR2 junction there's
an indistinct, difficult-to-spot footpath signed 'canyon-
ing entrada', heading steeply up on the right at an acute

angle. Follow this narrow, slippery path for about 200 metres to a wooden footbridge over the river.

Just after the bridge the path curves rightwards. Continue for 50 metres until just before a jumble of fractured rock, and take a small right-hand turn heading upriver, with the water to the right. Shortly afterwards take a left-hand turn, heading uphill and away from the river. This zigzags uphill to a **viewpoint**, then follow the main path as it zigzags down to a crossroads with a cart track.

Go left (PR7.2 goes right) to arrive at tarmac road, then turn left heading south-west. Follow the tarmac road past several viewpoints for the falls, and get back to the PR1/PR2 sign at the car park.

Walk the same footpath to the fork mentioned earlier (PR1/PR2 junction), and this time head right along PR2. Zigzag steeply up and then walk up along the ridge. ▸ This becomes a disused cart track heading south-west, fairly level initially then ascending slightly. Another cart track merges from the left about 1km from the PR1/PR2 junction; continue to a tarmac road and turn right. After 150 metres take a cart track heading acutely off to the left, nearly doubling back, signposted PR2.

Waymarkings are infrequent but there are some cairns.

A tree-lined path in the autumnal mountain woods

There are now some excellent views of the valley as you walk on a path built of huge slabs of granite. This leads to a cart track; turn left then immediately right onto a footpath. ◄ Go straight across at a crossroads 10mins later, then zigzag down to a junction with another cart track. Go right and downhill. The cart track leads to a tarmac road, where you turn left. Walk along the road for 100 metres and take the third right-hand downhill footpath, with a wall and building to its left.

Be careful not to follow PR7.1, which is also waymarked red/yellow.

Arrive at a crossroads with a cart track 10mins later, go straight ahead towards a ruined building, then curve slightly left past an old white building which was a **Matas Nacionais** (National Forest) building. Shortly after this is a T-junction with another cart track; turn left and go downhill, then turn immediately right onto a downhill footpath. This leads to the crossroads encountered at the beginning; go straight ahead and retrace steps back to the start.

WALK 23
*Rota do Glaciar,
Torre–Manteigas*

Start	Torre (N40°19.305′ W07°36.830′)
Finish	St Peter's Church, Manteigas (N40°24.026′ W07°32.382′)
Distance	18.5km
Total ascent	210m (with 1440m descent)
Grade	Difficult
Time	6½hrs
Terrain	Very tough rocky sections, some good footpaths, a section on quiet tarmac and dirt road to finish
Map	Adventure Maps Serra da Estrela; Carta Militar 1:50,000 sheets 17-II and 20-I, 1:25,000 sheets 213, 223 and 224
Refreshments	At start and finish
Toilets	At start, Covão d'Ametade and finish
Access	From Manteigas, take a taxi to Torre (pronounced 'tor').
Note	Very low temperatures possible at the summit well into spring; warm clothing recommended

This outstanding linear walk, based on PR6 Rota do Glaciar ('the glacier route'), is best done in fine weather in order to appreciate the stunning views from the highest point in mainland Portugal (Torre, Serra da Estrela, 1993m). Torre itself, crammed with a shopping centre selling regional cheeses, meats and Serra de Estrela fluffy toy dogs, is frankly a bit of an eyesore. However, Cântaro Raso (1916m) is the antidote: clean, pristine and a place to enjoy the solitude (note that this part is not waymarked but it is an easy-to-follow path).

There is much to appreciate on this walk: Torre, a summit with a cairn circle, the carved monument of Senhora da Boa Estrela, cows grazing on the beautiful plateau of Nave de Santo António, waterfalls, stone houses, fountains, *termas* (spas), a trout farm, and Rio Zêzere running along the typical U-shaped glacier valley.

It may seem tempting to make this a there-and-back route, but even without the ascent this is a tough hike, walking on difficult rocky sections, and it takes significantly longer than you would imagine (even without extra time to admire the views).

> **The Torre** (Tower) summit is 1993m. King João IV, unsatisfied with its height, ordered the construction of a tower to raise the peak's height to 2000m – hence the name of this point.

Facing the tower, turn left and head south towards the radar dome (the left-hand one with GNR written on it), and then pass it on its left before turning east. Follow this indistinct path (marked with some cairns) as it heads downhill, curving to the left.

When you can see a **ruined building** (which was the cable car station) high up on the left, and the route is in a hollow with a tarn, there's a fork on the footpath. Go left and then down the valley, keeping the ruin to the left, to arrive at a tarmac road approximately 1km from the start of the walk.

Cântaro Raso (Shallow Jug) is visible ahead with a circle of tall thin cairns. Go straight over the tarmac road (the official route goes right, down the tarmac road), take any of the myriad faint trails heading east, and ascend to **Cântaro Raso** after 500 metres.

After enjoying the peace and the impressive views, retrace steps to the tarmac road. Turn left and walk downhill (it may be more comfortable to walk on the grass to the left of the road) until there's a small car park on the left. Walk down some steps to **Nossa Senhora da Boa Estrela**.

map continues on page 156

Our Lady of the Good Star is the patron saint of the shepherds. The impressive 1940s sculpture, over 7 metres high, is embedded in the rock. There will be a lot of visitors on her festive day: the second Sunday of August each year.

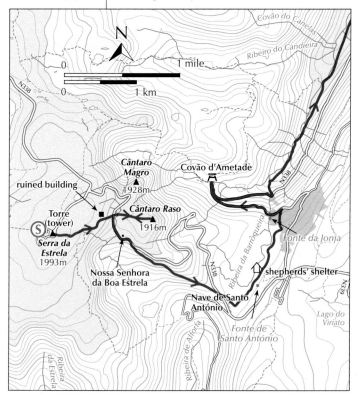

After admiring the sculpture, return to the road and follow it down to a small car park/passing place on the right-hand side. Go to the outer side of the crash barrier and walk just below and next to the right-hand side of the road. After 150 metres, take an uneven narrow footpath going off to the right just after a culvert. This section is very tough and uneven but has great views, with slow progress for 1.5km leading to a tarmac road. Go straight across via a gap in the crash barrier to descend to the plain of **Nave de Santo António**.

Nossa Senhora da Boa Estrela

Meet a cart track after 200 metres and follow it to curve round the plain, heading north-east. ▶ The track goes past a small open-air chapel, **Fonte de Santo Antonio** (fountain), and a **shepherds' shelter** (still open for use in bad weather).

This is a beautiful section, with massive boulders, heathers, hills and mountains as far as the eye can see.

Towards the end of this plateau the route becomes a stone path heading north-east in a lovely wooded section, and then by a particularly huge boulder on the left take a footpath that is easy to miss (if missed, there's a tarmac road in 200 metres; retrace steps from there). Follow this attractive downhill footpath for 350 metres through woods to a tarmac road, then turn left and continue going downhill.

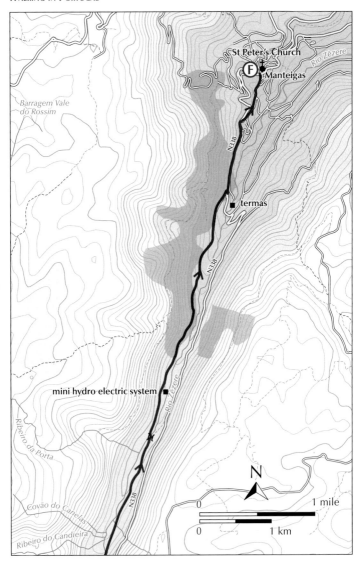

Go past **Fonte da Jonja** (fountain) and reach **Covão d'Ametade** (which has a picnic area and toilet) on a hairpin bend after just under 1.5km on the tarmac road. Continue on the tarmac road, now following red/white/yellow waymarkings. ▶ At the second bridge over a stream, 1km from the picnic area, take a clearly waymarked footpath on the left just after the crash barrier. This descends to the floor of the amazingly straight glaciated valley. Walk on the right side of **Rio Zêzere**.

The route is now joined by GR33.

Walk along for 3.5km and then cross the second **bridge** over Rio Zêzere – a concrete one signposted GR33 (no red/yellow waymarking) – then continue along a wide dirt road on the other side of river. Walk past a *levada* (water channel) and a **mini hydroelectric system**,

The Zêzere glacial valley, with Manteigas in the far distance

157

until the route becomes cobbled and arrives at a tarmac road (about 3.5km from the bridge).

Turn left and go downhill, walk past the *termas* (spa), and 500 metres later take the second turning on the right onto a cobbled road. Shortly afterwards, ignore an unhelpful sign saying turn right.

At the end of the 250-metre-long cobbled road, arrive at a tarmac road and turn right (downhill), and then immediately turn left onto another cobbled road. After 200 metres reach another tarmac road and turn right, still heading downhill, following just red/white waymarking to a car park area. Here the route turns left, signposted 'Centro Manteigas' (GR33 goes right).

Arrive at a roundabout a couple of minutes later and go right. This leads to a bigger tarmac road; go left and uphill, heading to the finish – **St Peter's Church** (Igreja de São Pedro) at the corner of Rua 1° de Maio and Rua Padre António Tarrinha.

WALK 24

Poios Brancos, Manteigas

Start/Finish	N338 near Covão d'Ametade (N40°19.606′ W07°34.236′)
Distance	8km
Total ascent	330m
Grade	Easy
Time	3hrs
Terrain	Mostly footpaths; some dirt road at beginning and a little tarmac at the end
Map	Adventure Maps Serra da Estrela; Carta Militar 1:50,000 sheets 20-I, 1:25,000 sheets 223 and 224
Access	On the N338 to Torre from Manteigas there's a left-hand dirt road 1.7km past Covão d'Ametade, signposted Poço do Inferno and Serra de Bo, with a board for PR7 at the start.
Parking	At start

PR7 Poios Brancos ('the white hill walk') is a delightful little hike with much to recommend it. The route begins at a significant altitude and ascends further via infrequently used paths to a rarely visited summit, Poios Brancos (1704m), giving views not just of the glacial valley but also a panorama of the massif (Walks 21 and 23). The last section is along the grass-covered sward of Nave de Santo António, ending with a woodland stroll. This is best done in good weather to appreciate the vistas.

Begin by walking north-east along the dirt road for 2km. Once out of the trees, turn right onto a wide footpath

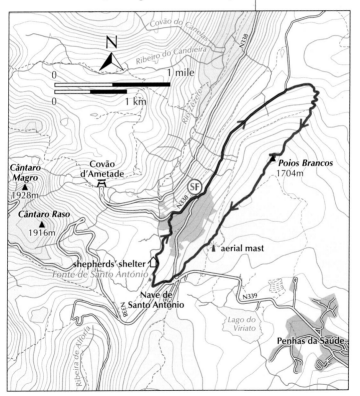

Walking among a plethora of flowers towards the summit of Poios Brancos with views of the jugs (granitic prominences) surrounding Torre

At several points of the walk the route is marked by a line of cairns. However, there are cairns everywhere so they are not completely reliable.

going uphill, signed PR7. Take a very indistinct footpath on the left after 850 metres; it's at the point when the footpath stops zigzagging up and is just gently ascending in a straight line. ◄

This next section is very indistinct. To the south-west is a gap like a saddle between two peaks; the route is towards the rightmost of those two peaks, following a line of cairns with some yellow/red waymarking for about 1.5km. Once at the crest strewn with stacked huge granite boulders, walk along it towards the summit of **Poios Brancos** marked with a black/white trig point (the official PR route does not go to the summit).

> **Poio** means 'hill', here referring to the granitic aggregation at the mountaintop. The people of Manteigas knew that winter had arrived when this point was covered in snow.

Return to the official path and head south-west, still following a line of cairns. This footpath meets a rough cart track after 600 metres; go right. Arrive at a T-junction with another rough cart track after 650 metres and go

straight across it onto an indistinct footpath along a line of cairns, heading towards a big red **aerial mast**. About 350 metres later go straight over another cart track and continue on the footpath for a further 750 metres to reach a tarmac road (there is a roundabout to the left). Go straight across the road and take a footpath signed for **Nave de Santo António**.

Line of cairns delineating the route on the flower-carpeted slope with heather, gorse and broom

> The **nave** is a very important meadow for the cows and sheep grazing here in spring and summer; they benefit from the purity and goodness of the grass, and their milk and meat can allegedly cure diseases. That is the likely origin of the association with St Anthony of Padua, who was Portuguese by origin and famous for his devotion to the sick. In the 18th century there was a hermitage dedicated to the saint in this meadow.

At the nave, with **Fonte de Santo António** (fountain) on the left, turn right and head towards the **shepherds' shelter**. After 500 metres, towards the end of this plateau, the route becomes a stone path heading north-east in a

The shepherds' shelter in the idyllic plain of Nave de Santo António

lovely wooded section, and then by a particularly huge boulder on the left take a footpath that's easy to miss (if missed, there's a tarmac road in 200 metres; retrace steps from there). Follow this attractive downhill footpath through woods for 350 metres to a tarmac road, then turn right (uphill) and continue back to the start.

AROUND LISBON

The Castle of the Moors, Sintra

This chapter comprises a handful of areas that are within easy reach of Lisbon. To the north-east is Aire e Candeeiros Nature Park, in the Estremadura region, only 1½hrs away from Lisbon. It is predominantly a limestone massif formed in the Jurassic period, encompassing Serra de Aire ('mountains of the air') in the north-east and Serra dos Candeeiros ('mountains of the lamps') in the west. What lie between these are not glaciated valleys but massive fractures: water flows through an intricate underground network, creating the area's famous cathedral-like caves – including the largest cave in Portugal, Grutas de Mira de Aire.

The maze-like traditional low stone walls found throughout the landscape have an almost organic, cellular curving pattern from an aerial view. The area is also famous for its 175 million-year-old dinosaur foot-prints (the world's oldest tracks), its medieval castles, and the UNESCO-listed monasteries of Alcobaça and Batalha.

To the north-west is Sintra-Cascais Nature Park, stretching across Serra de Sintra southwards to Cascais. A large part of the area is classified as UNESCO World Heritage cultural landscape, owing to the many splendid buildings from the era when the Portuguese royal family used it as their summer escape from the heat.

The coast provides an interesting terrain for hiking with cliffs over 100 metres high, golden sand beaches,

Cabo Espichel, Arrábida (Walk 28)

and a diversity of habitats for wildlife and vegetation. A stroll around the Palácio Nacional, Castelo dos Mouros (Moorish castle), Palácio da Pena, and Convento dos Capuchos are all highly recommended.

To the south, the Nature Park of Arrábida is only 30 minutes from Lisbon and it stretches over the south-western coast of the Setubal peninsula. The area provides splendid coastal views with sea cliffs, white sand beaches, sea birds, lighthouses and dinosaur footprints (Walk 28).

BASES

The start points for Walks 25–28 are all within 1½hrs drive from Lisbon, making it a convenient base to explore the area from – especially as it is easily accessible with its international airport. There is also accommodation available at the start of Walk 25, in Alvados. For Walk 26, the nearest accommodation would be the nearby village of Alcobertas. There are plenty of choices for both accommodation and restaurants in the Sintra and Arrábida areas, all within driving distance of the start of Walks 27 and 28.

WALK 25
Castelejo, Alvados

Start/Finish	Junta de Freguesia Alvados (parish council building), Alvados (N39°32.934' W08°46.218')
Distance	13km
Total ascent	410m
Grade	Medium
Time	4½hrs
Terrain	Good footpaths and cart tracks
Map	Carta Militar 1:50,000 sheet 27-4, 1:25,000 sheet 318
Refreshments	No café on route but shop in Alvados
Access	Alvados is on the N243 between Porto de Mós and Mira de Aire. Follow signs to Junta de Freguesia, which is on Rua do Vale do Bispo.
Parking	At start

The PR5 Castelejo is named after the rocky hill in Aire e Candeeiros Nature Park that this walk skirts around, although the majority of the route goes up and along Costa de Alvados, which was part of the coast epochs ago. The route begins along a lovely footpath through a wooded area, lined with vinca, stinking hellebores, salvia, hawthorn and other wildflowers. The walk then winds through the geologically fascinating landscape with a display of karst and limestone. A good ascent leads to the best-maintained set of the limestone walls that characterise this area, whose maze-like pattern makes navigation challenging.

Facing the Junta de Freguesia (parish council building) in Alvados, go left along the road towards a small chapel. Turn right just before it, along Rua Dom Fuas Roupinho. Walk along the tarmac road, reach a fork and go left, heading towards the imposing hill of Costa de Alvados. Arrive at another fork 50 metres later and go left. When the tarmac road turns 90° to the left, take a cart track on the right off the bend, heading towards the limestone

View of Castelejo from the top of Costa de Alvados

massif. This becomes a footpath winding through olive groves.

Continue to walk towards the limestone hills, soon arriving at a fork. Go right, heading west. Descend into the river valley and go up on the other side for 20 metres to arrive at a dirt road, then turn left. The route is in the gap between two imposing limestone hills: Castelejo on the left, and Costa do Alvados on the right, carved by Ribeiro da Canada.

After 1.5km on the dirt road, just after a breeze-block-built **shack**, the path forks. Go right on a cart track towards the impressive gully, then zigzag up past slabs of karst. Ignore any turnings until suddenly surrounded by walled paddocks and fields containing the ends of myriad limestone strata.

This is the vast **Planalto de Santo António**, the top of the Estremenho limestone massif formed in the middle Jurrassic period, which forms most of the nature park. Serra dos Candeeiros and Serra de Aire are part of the same massif.

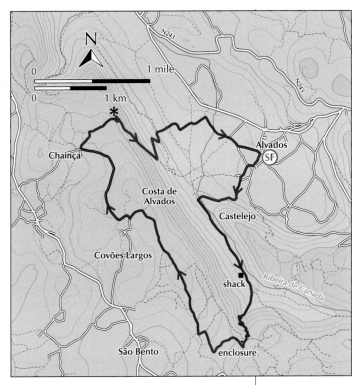

Continue following the cart track, passing many stone walls. When the cart track goes past a small round **enclosure** on the right with the rock strata on the left (about 1.25km from the shack), turn acutely right, heading north-west (straight ahead leads to a village).

Navigation becomes a bit more difficult in the next section. The route is between two walls and it curves left to head south-west. Shortly after this the walls flare apart; follow the right-hand wall to arrive, almost immediately, at a crossroads. Go straight ahead, walking over slabs of limestone pavement, and continue to follow the right-hand wall.

The route becomes a narrow cart track; follow it for 100 metres to a T-junction with a wider cart track and turn right, heading north-west. Ignoring any turnings, continue slightly uphill for 300 metres to another T-junction and turn left. After 100 metres arrive at an impressive collection of well-maintained limestone walls, and shortly afterwards turn right, leading to a major cart track heading north.

Follow this main track for 2km, descending to a crossroads. ◄ Turn left to a well-travelled path heading downhill (straight ahead is a dead-end). After 200 metres, pass some farm buildings, arrive at a T-junction with a major dirt road, and turn right (the road to the left leads to the village of Covões Largos).

There are two disused windmills and a massive quarry visible across the valley on the left.

Stay on the main dirt road for 1.5km and enter the village of **Chainça**. The dirt road becomes tarmac. Take the first right turn, back onto a dirt road, and immediately afterwards at a big triangular clearing the path forks; go right and then ignore the first right-hand turn. At the next fork go left, which leads to a T-junction with a cart track.

Admire the wind farm in Serra dos Candeeiros (Walk 26).

Turn right. ◄ Shortly afterwards go right at the next two forks, always heading north-east. When the path starts to descend you can appreciate the best **views** of the walk, overlooking the Depression of Alvados. On the left is the town Alcaria and on the right is Alvados.

> The **Depression of Alvados** is a low, flat area sandwiched between the St Anthony's Plateau to the south and the plateau of Sao Mamede to the north. The village is named after the depression. Since the 16th century it has been an important olive oil area; in 1559 it produced over 200,000 litres of olive oil.

About halfway down the descent (approximately 800 metres), turn acutely left onto an easily missed footpath and continue for 550 metres. Ignore a right-hand narrow footpath, then ignore another right-hand footpath off a bend, and turn right onto a cart track among the olive trees, heading north-east. Keep following the main path

for 200 metres to arrive at a crossroads/junction, then go right and immediate left.

Continue for a further 250 metres to a T-junction with a dirt road and turn right towards Alvados. Go straight ahead at a crossroads after 500 metres, then go underneath a wooden bridge (which seems to have no function). Arrive at a big tarmac clearing with a football/ recreational club on the left, and continue straight ahead along Rua da Cova do Morto. ▶ Go left at the next fork, walk along Rua Das Mangas to a T-junction and turn right, which leads back to the start in **Alvados**.

Olive trees with the massif of Castelejo in the background

This translates as 'road of the pit of the dead'.

WALK 26
Chãos

Start/Finish	Weaving centre, Chãos (N39°25.029' W08°55.222')
Distance	15km
Total ascent	460m
Grade	Medium
Time	5hrs
Terrain	A combination of good footpaths and cart tracks
Map	Carta Militar 1:50,000 sheet 26-2, 1:25,000 sheet 327
Toilets	At weaving centre when open. Also in building opposite picnic area at Olho de Água.
Access	From Alcobertas, south of the nature park, follow Rua do Olho de Água which becomes Estrada do Barco. Take the first left onto Rua São Francisco de Assis. This passes through Chãos; at its end, a small dirt road on the left, Rua de Escolar, leads to the weaving centre.
Parking	At weaving centre
Note	In summer the steep ascent leading to Casais Monizes is best done earlier in the day before it gets too hot.

PR2 (waymarked red/yellow) is a must-do in the Aire e Candeeiros Nature Park. The walk goes past old and new windmills and up to one of the highest points in the nature park: Candeeiros summit (497m). It provides stupendous panoramic vistas from the 5km crest, with views of limestone cliffs and the area's characteristic stone walls, encapsulating the unique limestone environment of this area.

On the official version of this route there's a variant to walk through the town of Alcobertas, but the route described here is more attractive and shorter.

Walk from the weaving centre along the dirt road back towards Chãos, which becomes Rua São Francisco de Assis. When the dirt road becomes tarmac, turn immediately left before entering the village. Go along a cart track running inside a little olive grove, and then past a long white building.

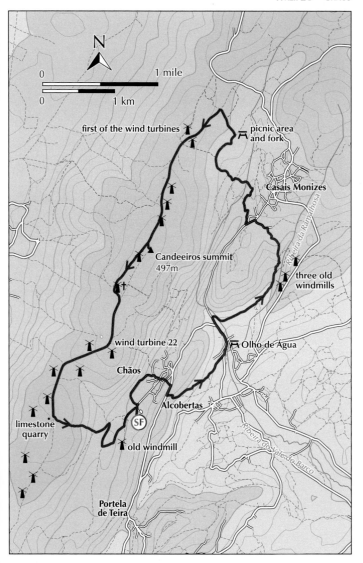

N

0 _____ 1 mile
0 _____ 1 km

first of the wind turbines

picnic area and fork

Casais Monizes

Candeeiros summit
497m

three old windmills

wind turbine 22

Chãos

Olho de Água

SF

Alcobertas

limestone quarry

old windmill

Portela de Teira

Ribeira da Ramalhosa

Ribeira do Vale do Barco

At the end of the building, join a dirt track which becomes a tarmac road, and then arrive at a T-junction with Rua das Oliveirinhas. Turn right, go across one crossroads (be careful not to follow the red/yellow way-markings of PR4) and take the next left, Rua do Moinho.

Take the first right into Rua Curral Mota, go immediately left at the next junction, and then take the very first right which is a cart track heading downhill, just after a drive for a house. After 20m, take the downhill footpath forking off left, just before reaching some buildings. This leads to a tarmac road in 100 metres; go right and downhill, and then take a left-hand cart track just before a large round white and blue building.

After 200 metres arrive at a fork for variants 'A' and 'B'; go left, signposted for Olho de Água, and continue along a cart track through olive groves for just under 1km. Ignore all turnings until the track reaches a tarmac road, then turn left. There's a **picnic area** on the right 150 metres further along, and a white building (toilets available) straight ahead. Fork left and go along Estrada do Barco, keeping the white building to the right and following signs for 'Fonte de Chãos PR2'.

The mosaic sign for the picnic area at Olho de Água

About 300 metres along, take the first right-hand fork into a dirt road, level at first then going up in the direction of some wind turbines. Just over 100 metres later turn right, heading north-west, and continue along this main cart track for 1.2km as it becomes a footpath. ▶ Beneath the looming escarpment, turn left across naked limestone, now heading north, and ascend steeply uphill and away from the cliffs.

Arrive at a T-junction with another footpath and turn left uphill. The footpath is now next to fields and between two limestone walls, at the end of which it reaches a T-junction with a cart track. Turn left, heading slightly downhill. This becomes a tarmac road on the outskirts of **Casais Monizes** village.

Reach a T-junction with another tarmac road, Rua Principal Sul, and turn left (slightly downhill). Go straight ahead past the last building in the village, where this tarmac road becomes a dirt track, and turn immediately right (uphill).

After 400 metres take a footpath on the right (the main dirt track turns 90° left), with the wind turbines in the distance on the left and a big quarry uphill to the right. Immediately fork right with a ruined building on the left. The footpath then joins another one coming in from the right, and then curves left to go between two fields with limestone walls. After 150 metres, at the end of the walls, take the route curving left uphill. This leads to a T-junction with a dirt road; turn left and uphill towards the wind turbines. Shortly afterwards arrive at a T-junction with another dirt road; turn right and go slightly uphill.

Continue on the main path for about 900 metres, ignoring any turnings, and arrive at a lovely **picnic area** where there's a big fork. Fork left and there are more picnic tables to the right. After 400 metres, fork left again and immediately turn left, heading to the **wind turbines**.

From ancient times, **windmills** used to top every crest in this area. The uninterrupted air currents which give their name to Serra de Aire used to provide power for the milling of grain. Today they power

To the right are fascinating limestone cliffs, on top of which are the remains of three of the many windmills that used to dot this area.

a wind farm with 37 turbines, providing 111,000 kilowatts, which is enough for 70,000 homes.

Ignore the service road to each of these turbines and continue along the main dirt road that tops the 5km-long crest that is the high point of this walk.

The **views** from the crest are vast: to the north-east lies the main portion of the limestone massif that forms the nature park; south is Rio Maior; and on clear days you can see the Atlantic Ocean 10km to the north-west.

At wind turbine 22 there's an optional shortcut on the left, signposted PR4, which leads to Chãos.

Reach a huge trig point and branch left (straight ahead) to **Candeeiros summit**, then retrace steps to the main route and turn left. Continue past a **cross** on the left, and after 100 metres fork left onto a cart track. Follow this for 300 metres to a T-junction with the main dirt track and turn right. ◄ Continue for 2km to a major **limestone quarry** on the right and take a faint footpath turning left, marked with red/yellow on posts. (If the turning is missed you'll come to the end of the quarry where there's a radio mast.)

The path becomes slightly indistinct but is way-marked infrequently by red/yellow on posts. It continues to descend for 700 metres down the valley, heading east, and arrives at a dirt road. Turn left and downhill, and at the next crossroads take the right-hand turn nearly doubling back. (Caution required at the crossroads as there are red/yellow waymarkings for PR4.) Take the first left-hand cart track, after 300 metres, which leads to an **old windmill**.

Here turn 90° degrees left towards Chãos. The path is indistinct again, marked with red/yellow on posts, but if these have fallen over just walk in a straight line to a dirt road ahead, then turn left (north) towards the village. The dirt road merges with a major dirt road, and as it approaches the village the weaving centre/start is on the right-hand side.

WALK 27

Peninha, Sintra

Start/Finish	Santuário da Peninha car park (N38°46.157′ W09°27.531′)
Distance	5km
Total ascent	175m
Grade	Easy
Time	2hrs
Terrain	Cart tracks and a good forest footpath
Map	Adventure Maps Sintra-Cascais; Carta Militar 1:50,000 sheet 34-4, 1:25,000 sheet 415
Access	On the N247 between Malveira de Serra and Colares there's a west-facing turn signposted for the *santuário* (sanctuary).
Parking	At start

This is a lovely little walk in the Sintra-Cascais Nature Park. Based on PR10 (waymarked red/yellow), the route described here features an extra little section to avoid retracing steps after exploring the megalithic monument of Adrenunes. En route, you get to stroll through some fine woodland footpaths and see the Pedras Irmãs ('sisters stones'), a mountain-top chapel and a ruined hermitage.

Start the walk from the parking area by heading southwest towards the sanctuary. About 150 metres up the hill, fork left. ▶ Walk past **Ermida de São Saturnino** on the right.

The site of the **St Saturnino chapel** was a Visigoth sacred plot around the fifth to eighth century AD. Over the years several apparitions of Our Lady, including one to a mute shepherd girl who consequently regained her speech, led to the building of the subsequent chapels.

Fork right to explore the Capela da Peninha at the summit and its viewpoint; Cabo da Roca, the westernmost point of continental Europe is visible.

*Santuário da Peninha,
composed of
Capela da Peninha
and Ermida de
São Saturnino*

Take the footpath that turns 90° to the right (at the point where the dirt path turns 90° left and downhill), heading north-west towards a copse of trees. Follow this beautiful footpath for 450 metres through the woods downhill, then reach a dirt road and turn right, going slightly uphill initially. This leads to a tarmac road after 600 metres; go straight across onto an indistinct path, heading north-west.

Go through a picnic area and 150 metres later meet a cart track at a crossroads and turn left (the footpath straight ahead is the return route). Next take the first right-hand footpath, which is waymarked and slightly uphill. At the next fork, go left (do not go downhill), which leads to **Adrenunes** in 200 metres.

> **Adrenunes** is a prehistoric megalithic structure of several huge boulders with a 5m-high passage. It was thought to be a dolmen but recent excavation did not reveal any evidence of funerary use. At an altitude of 426m, it provides superb views of Cabo da Roca and the mountain range of Sintra.

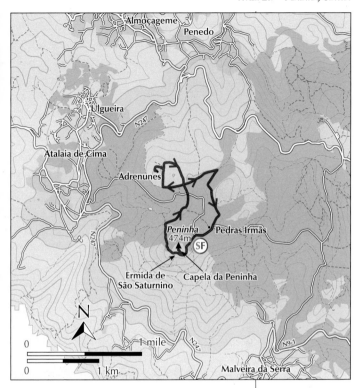

Retrace steps to the previous fork, this time going downhill, then fork right almost straight away. This leads back to the crossroads mentioned earlier. Now turn left to continue the route, heading north-east.

After 500 metres reach a T-junction with cart track and go right, slightly uphill, almost doubling back. This leads to a tarmac road; turn right. ▶ Take the first left turn, signposted PR10 (also a brown sign for Santuário da Peninha), back to the start.

The impressive Pedras Irmãs are on the right and there's a picnic area.

WALK 28
Cabo Espichel, Arrábida

Start/Finish	Santuário de Cabo Espichel (Our Lady of the Cape Sanctuary) (N38°25.231' W09°12.814')
Distance	10.5km
Total ascent	450m
Grade	Medium
Time	4hrs
Terrain	Footpaths
Map	Adventure Maps Arrábida; Carta Militar 1:50,000 sheet 38-1, 1:25,000 sheet 464
Refreshments	Café at sanctuary
Toilets	At sanctuary
Access	Drive to the very end of N379 from Sesimbra
Parking	At sanctuary
Note	GPS (plus map and compass) recommended

This is Arrábida Nature Park's westernmost extent, in a geologically fascinating area with a unique ecosystem. The route's highlights include a sanctuary, two sets of dinosaur footprints, some fantastic coastline, a ruined fort and a lighthouse.

There is an unusual navigation hazard in the form of a plethora of routes: the walk includes most of PR1 (Maravilhas do Cabo, 'wonders of the cape') and PR2 (Chã dos Navegantes, 'level area of the navigators'), plus a section of the GR11, which goes all the way to Santiago, Spain. Waymarking is infrequent and care must be taken to stick to the described route.

The Casa da Água (House of Water) is the end of an aqueduct which used to supply water to the sanctuary.

From the sanctuary, head east along a little ffotpath to the left of the Casa da Água. ◄ Continue for 500 metres, with multi-coloured sandstone cliffs to the left, to reach a cart track. Turn left and downhill to follow PR2 with red/yellow waymarking. Continue on the main path for about 1km to reach the **viewpoint for the Pedra da Mua dinosaur footprints**.

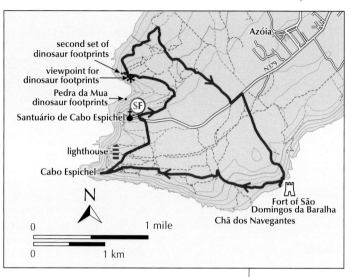

Legend has it that the **footprints** were left by a giant donkey carrying Our Lady of the Cape, whose apparition to two old men in 1215 eventually led to the building of the sanctuary of the same name. The true story, that these are the 160 million-year-old tracks of a group of 37 sauropods, is just as captivating.

Santuário de Cabo Espichel

179

Take care when visiting the dinosaur footprints as the cliff is very crumbly.

After admiring this set of footprints, take a footpath at the far left of the railings for 200 metres to explore a **second set of dinosaur footprints**. ◄

Afterwards, return to the main path and head northwest. There's a plethora of paths; keep an eye out for waymarking, but if absent, follow a main cart track which curves right at its end, following the coastline overlooking Lisbon and Costa Caparica, now heading north-east. This leads to a crossroads about 1km later; turn right (GR11 goes left, waymarked red/white), following the signposted PR2 and going away from the coast.

After 500 metres, at a multi-way junction with about five options, take the middle, signposted one, heading south-east. Arrive at a tarmac road after about 1km and turn left towards the town of Azóia, parting company with PR2.

The Santuário; below are the Pedra da Mua dinosaur footprints, but you really have to be there to appreciate them

Walk along the road for 200 metres then turn right; there's a large sign here for PR1 (the 'no entry' sign is for cars, not walkers). After 900 metres take the second, well-signposted right-hand fork; the route then becomes a narrow footpath heading downwards for 500 metres to the disused **Fort of São Domingos da Baralha**.

Built in 1665, the **Fort of São Domingos da Baralha** contains the ruins of Capela do Senhor Jesus dos Navegantes (chapel). It was abandoned after the 19th-century Portuguese Civil War.

After exploring the ruins, go back to the footpath and turn left to head west, following the red/white/yellow waymarking of PR1 and GR11.

The **rock** here is limestone and karst, sculpted by water and waves, and is very different from the north side of the peninsula. This flatter area is the Chã dos Navegantes – a marine terrace in the last interglacial period.

This leads, after 900 metres, to a T-junction with a bigger footpath; turn right and uphill. Some 300 metres along this path, which has a reasonably steep ascent, turn left following GR11 (PR1 goes straight ahead). The route then curves right (do not take a faint footpath straight ahead). There are multiple paths with infrequent way-marking, making navigation quite difficult. Take any path

The lighthouse of Cabo Espichel

that heads west towards Cabo Espichel, a small group of buildings to the left of the lighthouse.

Eventually, 2km after the fort, arrive at a T-junction and go right, uphill. Turn left almost immediately, heading west again towards Cabo Espichel, about 1km away. Arrive at **Cabo**, marked by ruined buildings and gun emplacements.

> **Cabo** is the westernmost point of the nature park and provides excellent views of the multiple strata of sandstone upon which the lighthouse stands.

From there, take any path to the **lighthouse**, followed by any of the multiple paths leading back to the **sanctuary** and the start.

TEJO AND SÃO MAMEDE NATURE PARKS

Across the plain to the mountain ranges of both Portugal and Spain north of Salvaterra do Extremo (Walk 29)

Tejo International Nature Park extends along both the Portuguese and Spanish sides of the Rio Tejo. The major attractions of the area are the exceptional vistas and the raptors; you may be lucky enough to spot a black vulture (these are on the International Union for Conservation of Nature (IUCN) 'Red List'). The symbol of the park is the black stork: rarer, smaller, shier and more wary than its ubiquitous white counterpart. Another highlight is Tejo's wines, which are some of the best in Portugal, arguably surpassing even Douro's.

Serra de São Mamede Nature Park, created only in 1989, is an undiscovered natural beauty. The highest peak in the area is, naturally enough, São Mamede (1025m), but it is not included in the walks here. Not only is it populated with radio masts, but everybody just drives there.

BASES

The capital of the area is the impossibly pretty double-walled town of Marvão (Walk 31), where there is accommodation available. Nearby are Idanha-a-Velha (a beautiful yet quiet town with Roman history, medieval walls and a Visigoth cathedral) and Monsanto (once voted the 'most Portuguese town in Portugal', and the site of an amazing Knights Templar castle with fantastic views), both well worth visiting. Accommodation is also available at the start of Walk 29 in the small town of Salvaterra do Extremo, and in Portagem at the start of Walk 31.

WALK 29

Rota dos Abutres, Salvaterra do Extremo

Start/Finish	Igreja Matriz de Misericordia (church), Salvaterra do Extremo (N39°53.008′ W06°54.847′)
Distance	11.5km
Total ascent	275m
Grade	Medium
Time	4hrs
Terrain	Almost all off-road, with a short section along a quiet tarmac road
Map	Carta Militar 1:50,000 sheet 25-1, 1:25,000 sheet 283
Refreshments	Café at start
Toilets	At start
Access	Salvaterra do Extremo is on the N332-4, which is a turning from the N240. The church is on the main road.
Parking	At start

PR1 Rota dos Abutres ('the route of the vultures') goes all the way down to the Rio Erges, with views of the romantic ruins of Castillo Peñafiel (which is in Spain: the river forms the boundary between Portugal and Spain). Beginning on a lovely ancient *calçada* (stone-built pavement) between two walls, the route takes in an observatory where the number of raptors to be seen is impressive, as is the profusion of wildflowers by the riverbank.

The best time of the year for this walk is spring when the river is high and the wildflowers are at their peak (although you might find yourself battling through the deep grass of a wildflower meadow). Alternatively autumn, when the fields are golden and the river is a dry desert of smoothed pebbles, is a pleasing option.

Start directly behind the church, heading south-east along a little cobbled road (waymarkings are infrequent in the town), then take the second left-hand turn with house number 33 on the corner. Continue down this path, walking between two walls, and pass two **chafurdãos** (circular structures whose purpose is unknown).

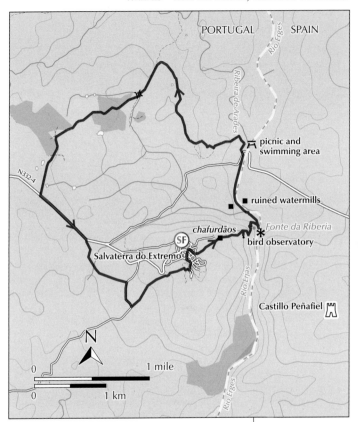

When the walls separate, follow the left-hand wall. The path then forks by a ruined building; the main route goes left and downhill, but following the right-hand fork to the **bird observatory** is highly recommended. ▶

Here you can look for vultures and enjoy the view of the crenellated Castillo Peñafiel.

Raptors found in this area include the black vulture, golden eagle, griffon vulture and Egyptian vulture. The black vulture, with a wingspan up to 3 metres, is one of the largest birds of prey in the world.

Walking through golden grasses below the Spanish Castillo Peñafiel

The route goes through two gates and passes the **Fonte da Ribeira** (spring); make a short detour downwards on the right to a **viewpoint** for the castle, birds, gorge and raging torrent.

Afterwards continue on this side of the river, following the path upstream. Pass a **ruined watermill** (another one on the other side of the river), and after 300 metres go up a set of rough steps on the left with wooden hand railing. Walk along this higher path, which then descends. Continue for another 500 metres and arrive at a tarmac road with a low bridge across the river leading to a bar on the Spanish side (open seasonally only). From the bridge, walk away from Spain, with a **picnic and swimming area** on the right. The road curves to the left; take the first right to a gravelled area and go along a cart track, heading north initially.

After 700 metres take the second turning on the right – a very indistinct cart track – and then 100 metres

Waymarkings are infrequent in this section.

later take another turning to the right. ◄ Reach a more main cart track and turn right. Continue for 450 metres, ignoring any turnings and going through a rudimentary gate which is there to stop animals only, to arrive at a

T-junction with a more main cart track. Take a signposted left turn and go over another gate, now heading south-west. After 500 metres cross a little stream via a tiny **bridge**, leading to a fork. Go right and continue heading south-west.

The Rio Erges with Castillo Peñafiel just visible across the border

Follow the main path for about 2km and then turn left at a T-junction with a tarmac road (**N332-4**). Walk along for 900 metres and take the first right, which is a dirt road. Then take the first left, which is a hardly used cart track with a gate on the corner. Reach a tarmac road and turn right; this heads away from the town Salvaterra do Extremo, but is the correct route. When the tarmac road curves hard to the right 350 metres later, take a cobbled road to the left. After a further 650 metres, at a T-junction with another road, turn right and continue uphill.

When this road ends in 300 metres, turn right at a T-junction with tarmac, then first left, now on cobbles. Next take the first right, then the first left and first left again by Casa do Forno (hotel). Then take the first right to the town pillory on Largo da Praça. Go across this small square, then turn right and walk along Rua Joaquim M. Lopes Dias, leading back to the start.

WALK 30

GR29 Rota dos Veados

Start/Finish	Polydesportivo (sports centre) in Rosmaninhal (N39°43.626' W07°05.547')
Distance	41km
Total ascent	1030m
Grade	Challenging
Time	13hrs (or 2 days)
Terrain	Almost all on dirt roads
Map	Carta Militar 1:50,000 sheet 25-III, 1:25,000 sheet 306
Refreshments	Cafés in Rosmaninhal
Access	From Castelo Branco, drive east on N240 for 35km. Turn south onto N353, signposted Rosmaninhal, which is at the end of this road. Then follow the signs for the polydesportivo (a blue building just off Rua da Santa).
Parking	At start
Warning	This route involves river/stream crossings that may be difficult after heavy rain

GR29 encompasses the essence of Tejo International Nature Park, and is a *grande rota* (waymarked in red/white) that can be completed in one very long day or two shorter days. The big selling point of this walk is the extreme sense of unconstrained space, with vast horizons, huge vistas and complete solitude. It is called Rota dos Veados – 'route of the deer' – as there are so many to see. The bird observatory is the only official extra recommended here, as in addition to the large numbers of griffon vultures to be seen, it is also a superb (and the only) viewpoint for Rio Tejo, deep in the valley beneath.

FOR A TWO-DAY HIKE

A good way to split the walk is to overnight at Couto dos Correias. Accommodation close to the route is available at Casa dos Xarês (www. casadosxares.wixsite.com/info, tel +351 969 826 027) in Couto dos Correias, and also at Hotel Rural Herdade da Poupa in Rosmaninhal (www. herdadedapoupa.com, tel +351 961 557 899).

If staying at the above places, Rosmaninhal to Couto dos Correias is 24km, 570m ascent, 7½hrs, and Couto dos Correias to Rosmaninhal is 17km, 460m ascent, 5½hrs.

Alternatively, split the route into two circular day hikes (see below).

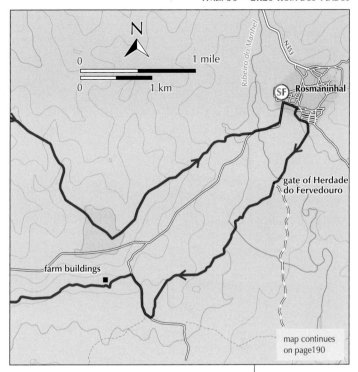

From the sports centre head east along the road, away from the sculpture of shepherd and sheep, signposted 'GR29 Ponte Longe'. ▸ Take the first right after passing the exercise park on the left. (Ignore the red/white cross; the official route goes through the park instead of staying on the road, which is not necessary.)

Waymarking is poor in town.

After 100 metres turn left at the end of the road, which then becomes a dirt road and forks. Go right and walk along a tarmac road with some houses to the left. Turn right and head south along a dirt road for 1km to the front **gate of Herdade do Fervedouro**.

Go straight ahead through a rudimentary gate (the main dirt road turns sharp left). About 750 metres later,

189

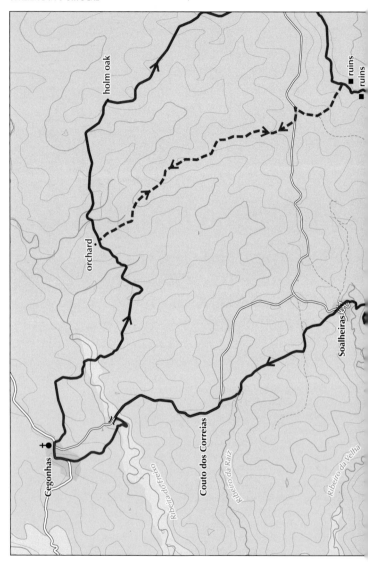

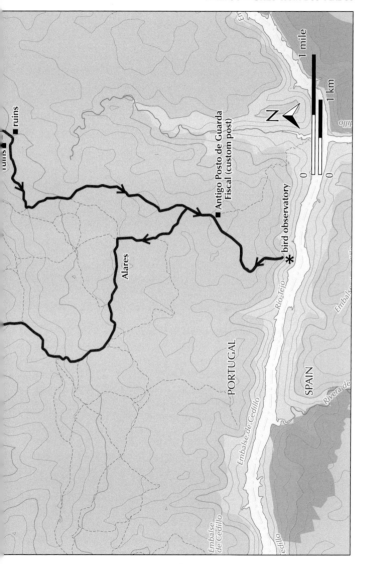

GR29 provides vistas of mountain ranges in both Portugal and Spain

This is the start/finish of the connecting section for the two circular day walks: turn right here if splitting the route into two (see below).

cross a fence via a stepladder, ford a stream, and then the cart track meets a dirt road at a T-junction 2.5km from the gate. Turn right; the route goes downhill initially then it heads uphill.

Halfway up this slope, about 650 metres from the T-junction, take a left-hand cart track that almost immediately goes underneath some power cables. The route then joins a bigger dirt road heading towards some buildings. At the **farm buildings** turn right to walk in between them, onto an indistinct cart track, heading west. Go into and out of a *barranco* (ravine), through a rudimentary gate, and reach a junction with a main cart track after just under 2km from the farm buildings. ◄

Turning left, go downhill and head towards a **ruined building**. Go past it to another ruined building with an interesting rounded end. Ignore a left-hand turn and arrive at a third ruined building where the navigation gets rather difficult. From this building, the route is a very indistinct path marked by a signpost heading west, towards a dried-out valley, leading to an ancient rudimentary **dam**. Stay on the left-hand side of the valley and walk downstream on a very indistinct path to a wall in front of a fourth ruined building. (If lost, from the third ruined building, head west for 75 metres to the dam then south-west for 150 metres to arrive at the wall.)

Stay to the left of this wall and walk along the bottom of the valley. Then cross over to the other side of the valley and head south-west towards a fifth ruined building, visible atop a rise on the right. On reaching it, turn right to head north-west in the direction of a sixth ruined building. Continue 100 metres then curve west (not actually reaching the sixth building), going past a very old untended olive grove. After 350 metres go straight ahead through one rudimentary gate, followed by another. The route reaches a major dirt road 500 metres later; turn left and downhill. Go left at the next fork, following a sign for Antigo Posto de Guarda Fiscal (custom post).

Ignore three turnings to the left and arrive at a big junction. Go straight ahead to follow the signposts for GR29.1 to Antigo Posto de Guarda Fiscal and GR29.2 to the bird observatory. Then fork right, and then left, onto a rough cart track. About 500 metres after the big junction, pass the **custom post** on the left.

There is a trig point up on the right; follow the main cart track for 800 metres, then turn right onto a faint footpath signposted for the bird observatory, heading due south. Follow this for 500 metres to the **viewpoint** at the end, with great views of the Rio Tejo, and good birdwatching opportunities.

> **Rio Tejo** at 1007km long is the longest river in the Iberian Peninsula, flowing through Spain (where it is called the Tagus) and Portugal. The source of the river is in the Albarracin mountain range; it runs along the border of the two countries for 47km and crosses the width of Portugal before emptying into the Atlantic Ocean near Lisbon.

After exploration, retrace steps to the big junction above, and follow a sign for GR29, heading north-west. Later ignore another signpost for GR29.1; it goes back to the custom post.

Walking through a wildflower meadow towards the eerie deserted village of Alares

Continue on the main track, which curves right going uphill. Just over 1km after the big junction, arrive at a crossroads with another cart track, next to a fence, and take the signposted left turn which is due west. Fork left by a pond 200 metres later. The waymarking here is poor. Walk between two walls for about 500 metres (if overgrown, walk to the side) and arrive at the ruined village of **Alares**.

> In 1865 Viscount Morão claimed ownership of a vast area including **Alares**, Cobeira and Cegonhas Velha, and the inhabitants started paying him rent. After the death of his son, confusion over ownership led to attacks by people from Rosmaninhal over the following 10 years, in what was known as the 'War of the Hills'. Eventually the government intervened in 1930, the people of Alares were relocated to Soalheiras, and the village was abandoned.

Go through Alares, exit on the western part and arrive at a T-junction with a cart track. Turn left, ignoring another path on the left signposted GR 29.1, and go straight ahead, signed 'Soalheiras 3.4km'. Ignoring all turnings, ascend for 1.5km and meet a big dirt road. Follow this to the right and continue the ascent.

At the top, the dirt road curves to the right, then go left at a fork. Follow the signposted main path to **Soalheiras**, then go up the main street through the town to the primary school and fork left, along Rua da Fonte, signposted for Couto dos Correias.

This road becomes a cart track; follow it to a T-junction with a more major dirt road and go left. Take an indistinct but signposted right-hand cart track 250 metres along the dirt road. Just over 1km later, at a T-junction with another cart track, go right and uphill. Reach a junction with a tarmac road, turn left and stay on it for 500 metres to arrive at **Couto dos Correias**. Walk through the village along the main road.

Stay on the tarmac road for 1km, and just before it crosses over a bridge take a signposted left-hand turn (Cegonhas is visible ahead up the hill). This leads to **Ribeira do Freixo**, which you then ford. (If the water is too high, cross the bridge and go all the way to Cegonhas on the tarmac road.)

About 100 metres from the river crossing, take an indistinct cart track curving right (north), which is not waymarked, for a good ascent with reasonable views. Follow it for 1km to arrive at **Cegonhas**. Go across the tarmacked Rua Nascente then fork right onto Rua António P Gardete, heading north. Turn right at the end of this road and reach the town **chapel**. ▶

This is the start point for the second circular day walk.

Take the first right-hand turn after the chapel, on a downhill cart track. Ignore any turnings and arrive at a fork after 1.5km; go right and downhill. Ford another section of **Ribeira do Freixo** (may be difficult after heavy rain). Reach a T-junction after 1.5km and go left, still on a cart track, and then ford another stream. Arrive at a crossroads with an **orchard** on the left. ▶

The connecting section for the two circular day walks runs south-east from here.

Go east, straight ahead, and continue down for 500 metres to ford two streams. After 1km meet a dirt road and turn right, going slightly uphill and heading due east initially. Ascend for 650 metres, then at a crossroads with a huge **holm oak**, turn right and uphill, signposted.

After 2.5km another path joins from the right; continue for 900 metres to another crossroads (there's a sign here for Monte do Vale Mosteiro). Turn left and then take a right-hand fork along a lesser-used cart track (just before the main dirt road curves left). It's not signposted but there are waymarkings further ahead.

A few minutes later the white town of Rosmaninhal is visible ahead. The cart track meets a tarmac road about 2km after the right-hand fork; turn left and downhill towards the town. Soon afterwards take a little footpath to the left of the road, which cuts a corner. This leads back to the same tarmac road further on; turn left and return to the start in **Rosmaninhal**.

TO TURN THIS ROUTE INTO TWO CIRCULAR DAY HIKES

Day 1 (21km, 460m ascent, 6½hrs)

Start from Rosmaninhal and follow the main route description as far as the junction with a main cart track beyond the farm buildings and *barranco* (ravine). Go right and uphill past a red/white cross (the GR route goes left and downhill). After 550 metres meet a more major dirt road and turn right, then reach a tarmac road 350 metres later and turn left. Take the second right-hand turn into a cart track, then 2km later go left at a fork and start going downhill. Reach a crossroads beside an orchard after 1.5km and turn right, heading east, and then follow the main walk above back to **Rosmaninhal**.

Day 2 (29km, 830m ascent, 9½hrs)

Start from the town chapel in Cegonhas (N39°44.331' W07°11.756') and follow the main route description as far as the crossroads with the orchard on the left (4km). Turn right, heading south-east, and reverse the section from the crossroads to the junction near the *barranco* on Day 1, above. On reaching the junction continue straight ahead (downhill) and follow the main route description to **Cegonhas**.

The connecting section

The connecting section between the crossroads and T-junction is not waymarked but it is an attractive section with good views of the mountain ranges in both Portugal and Spain.

WALK 31
Marvão

Start/Finish	Capela das Almas (chapel), Portagem (N39°23.037' W07°22.895')
Distance	8km
Total ascent	390m
Grade	Easy
Time	3hrs (not including exploring Marvão)
Terrain	Mostly on *calçada* (stone-built pavement), with some good footpath and a small amount of tarmac road. It is quite steep and the stone paths can be slippery if wet.
Map	Carta Militar 1:50,000 sheet 29-III, 1:25,000 sheet 348
Refreshments	In Portagem and Marvão
Toilets	In Portagem and Marvão
Access	Enter Portagem on the N246-1. Take the second exit at the main roundabout, then first right. The start is 150 metres on right.
Parking	At start

A real gem of a short walk. There are two different official versions of PR1, and this one wins the day. There are medieval tombs, a Roman bridge, ancient *calçada* and more besides. Marvão is an impossibly pretty and well-maintained double-walled town with a separate castle (small entry fee), well worth exploring. The views from the castle are breathtaking. There's even a reasonable amount of shade on the *calçada*, making it possible to do this walk when it's hot. A freshwater swim and a long lunch in town afterwards may be difficult to resist…

From the start, cross the wall on a set of steps between the chapel and the bridge, then walk over a little footbridge that crosses a stream and go along the bank of Rio Sever, heading south-west. Cross the footbridge that's beneath the road bridge (be careful not to follow the red/yellow waymarkings for PR5), then turn left to walk downstream along the riverbank. ▸ Walk past the **Toll Tower** on the

Decked and poplar tree-lined, this is the swimming area.

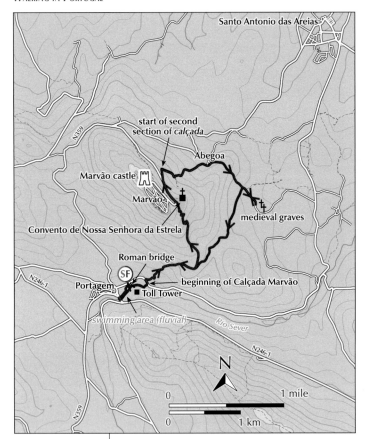

right and **Roman bridge** on the left, staying on this side of
the river and not crossing the bridge yet.

After 200 metres, cross over the river at the next footbridge and walk on cobbled road past what used to be
a watermill on the right (an old ruined-looking house).
Reach a tarmac road and go left. Take the first right 80
metres later to the **beginning of Calçada Marvão** (ancient
stone-built pavement).

The Roman bridge over Rio Sever (reconstructed in the 16th century)

Follow the *calçada* up for 2km, without deviation, to the top. Arrive at a tarmac road with **Convento de Nossa Senhora da Estrela** on the right and **Marvão** on the left. ▶

Marvão castle was built by King Dinis in the 13th century. It dominates the walled village that's perched on one of the highest crags of Serra da São Mamede (867m). The village was named after the eighth-century Islamic knight Ibn Marwan; the current medieval castle is at the site of his fort, where a Roman watchtower once stood, in an overpowering position overlooking Spain to its east. There are panoramic views of Serra da São Mamede, and on a clear day of Serra da Estrela; the highest mountains in Portugal. (Open 10am–5pm daily; www. cm-marvao.pt)

Go downhill on the tarmac road for about 300 metres and take the first right turn onto another *calçada*. Follow it for 800 metres to a shrine for Santa Teresinha do Menino Jesu in the village of **Abegoa**.

To explore Marvão, cross straight over the road and ascend to the town. There's a map of the town by the entrance through the walls.

Marvão castle atop precipitous cliffs

Turn right and walk along a tarmac road. (Do not take the *calçada* to the left.) This becomes a lovely footpath and 600 metres later arrives at a tarmac road. The route goes right, heading south-west, but first go left and walk down the tarmac road for 250 metres to see the **medieval graves** in the corner of a private field next to a farmhouse (viewed from fence).

Return to the main route and follow the main dirt road for just under 1km to an old farm building, then take the path that goes to the right of it. Continue straight ahead for 400 metres, heading south-west, back to **Calçada Marvão**. Retrace steps back to the **Roman bridge**, cross it and return to the start at **Portagem**.

MONSARAZ AND ÉVORA

The flooded landscape of Albufeira de Alqueva from the start point of Walk 33

The routes in this part of Alentejo ('beyond the Tejo') provide an opportunity to walk through history rather than focusing on nature and mountains.

Évora (Walk 32) was a Celtic town, then the Roman capital of the area, and in the 15th century it was the Portuguese royal residence. However, it is now smaller than it was in the medieval period. Its historic centre is UNESCO-listed, full of interesting architecture within its majestic city walls. Exploration is highly recommended.

The hill-top town of Monsaraz (Walk 33) has been inhabited since pre-history, as evidenced by the

megaliths that dot the surrounding plains, but it was then occupied by the Moors who named it after the gum rockrose (*sharish* in Arabic, *xarez* in Iberian), which is very common in this area. With a permanent population of only 20, it is now most visited as a viewpoint for the largest artificial lake in Europe.

BASES

Both Évora (Walk 32) and Monsaraz (Walk 33) are convenient bases from which to explore the area, with accommodation and restaurants widely available.

WALK 32
Évora aqueduct and Ecopista

Start/Finish	Car park on Avenida Condes Vilalva, Évora (N38°34.552', W07°54.869')
Distance	18.5km
Total ascent	210m
Grade	Medium
Time	5hrs
Terrain	Footpaths by the aqueduct for the first portion, some tarmac, then return via the Ecopista Ramal de Mora, a converted railway line
Map	Carta Militar 1:50,000 sheets 36-3 and 40-4, 1:25,000 sheets 448, 449 and 460
Refreshments	In Évora
Access	The car park is at the junction of Avenida Condes Vilalva and IP2, just outside the town walls and adjacent to a portion of the aqueduct.
Parking	At start

This fascinating route goes along the charmingly named Aqueduto da Água de Prata ('aqueduct of silver waters') deep into the surrounding countryside, where Montagu's harriers and storks soar over the verdant wildflower-rich landscape.

The 'unofficial' circular route described here joins together two easy-to-follow existing paths. The aqueduct is waymarked at times with a green triangle on white background, and the Ecopista is signposted in some places.

Walk along Avenida Condes Vilalva heading north-west, away from the centre of Évora, with the **Convento da Cartuxa** on the right. Take a footpath on the left just before the road goes beneath the aqueduct, which rises impressively on the right. This joins a dirt road 800 metres later, which then reaches a tarmac road, where you turn right. ◄

For a short time the route does not follow the exact course of the aqueduct.

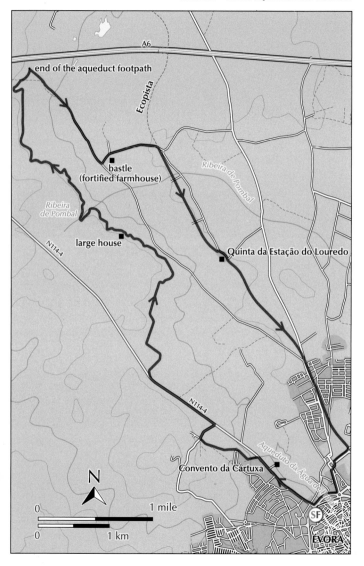

end of the aqueduct footpath

Ecopista

A6

Ribeira de Pombal

bastle
(fortified farmhouse)

Ribeira
de Pombal

large house

N114-4

Quinta da Estação do Louredo

N114-4

N

0   1 mile

0   1 km

Convento da Cártuxa

Aqueduto da Água

SF

ÉVORA

*The aqueduct with
Convento da Cartuxa
in the background*

The **aqueduct** was built of porphyritic granite from local quarries in 1530, when Évora was the second most important city in Portugal after Lisbon. In the late 19th century, as a result of not meeting the demands of the city and because the structure was in a ruined state, it was reconstructed and improved. The approximately 19km aqueduct still supplies water to the historic city, and was classified as a National Monument in 1910.

Arrive at the main road 250 metres later and turn left, heading away from Évora. When the aqueduct is visible again to the left and the road curves slightly rightwards, there's a footpath just before and inside of the crash barrier on the right-hand side of the road. Follow this footpath next to the aqueduct (which has crossed beneath the road) and go through a little gate under a bridge (not locked).

The footpath crosses over from the right to the left of the aqueduct on a bridge, and 100 metres later goes back to the original side at a **large house**. Walk on the house's drive for a few steps, then the aqueduct and the footpath veer left.

Walk over the **Ribeira de Pombal** on top of the aqueduct after 900 metres, and then the route turns right when the path is blocked by a fence after a further 600 metres. The path deviates from the aqueduct for a short time; walk along the fence line and then turn left at a cart track. Turn right 50 metres later, returning to the aqueduct. ▶

About 1.5km later it looks like you've reached the end of the aqueduct as it turns 90° right, but it's there underground. Continue between two wire fences and follow the line of pyramidal water access towers. At the end of the fenced section, continue heading north-east and cross over a cart track (the water access towers here are now domed). Arrive at the **end of the aqueduct footpath** after 200 metres, turn right and head south-east. ▶

The non-waymarked footpath becomes a cart track and then a tarmac road, always heading south-east, leading to a roundabout 1.5km from the end of the aqueduct footpath. Turn left, heading north-east. There is a **bastle** (fortified farm house) on the right-hand side. At the next roundabout, after 300 metres, go straight ahead, following signs for Ecopista on a very quiet tarmac road.

Continue for 700 metres and, just after a bus stop where there are railway tracks embedded into the tarmac, turn right and start walking on the very straight **Ecopista**. Follow this for 1.6km, ignoring all turnings until you reach **Quinta da Estação do Louredo** (a converted station); the path bypasses it by going round to the left of the building then back onto Ecopista.

Just under 2km later, go across a road, then go over a wooden bridge and the route becomes tarmac. Cross over two more tarmac roads and a dirt road. Leave the Ecopista by turning right at a roundabout, onto a footpath next to the road, following signs for 'Centro'.

After 300 metres cross to the left-hand side of the road just before the next roundabout, and take the first exit clockwise (left). Cross over the road again to be on the right-hand side, and at the next roundabout take the first exit anti-clockwise (right) to walk under the **aqueduct** back to the start.

At station number 12 the path is between the original 15th-century and 19th-century aqueducts.

The course of the aqueduct continues ahead, marked by cuboidal water access points but no pedestrian access.

WALK 33
Monsaraz

Start/Finish	Water cistern near Monsaraz town gate (N38°26.626′ W07°22.772′)
Distance	11km
Total ascent	230m
Grade	Easy
Time	3½hrs
Terrain	Mostly farm tracks, some tarmac
Map	Carta Militar 1:50,000 sheets 40-1 and 41-4, 1:25,000 sheet 474
Refreshments	Restaurants and cafés in Monsaraz; café in Telheiro
Toilets	Monsaraz (tourist office), Telheiro and Outeiro (by bus stop)
Access	The start point is a white domed structure south-east of the main town entrance, Porta da Vila.
Parking	Near start

This is the waymarked PR1 with a short diversion to Cromeleque do Xerez. There are great views of the drowned landscape of Albufeira de Alqueva and of majestic Monsaraz. The route may be short and not in the wild but it is nevertheless highly enjoyable, encompassing one of the best-preserved medieval towns in the region, two Neolithic monuments, and in season a variety of birds including storks and bee-eaters. The walk is short enough to begin or finish with lunch at Monsaraz, an impressive vantage point with panoramic views.

Monsaraz was occupied by the Moors for a few hundred years from the eighth century. It finally came under definitive Portuguese control in 1232 when it was re-conquered by King Sancho II and the Knights Templar. The town mosque was converted into a **cistern** in the 14th century to supply water for the town.

From the historic cistern, head north downhill in the direction of São Bento Chapel along Rua São João, and turn left at the end into a small square. Exit on the opposite side, head north-west and walk downhill along Rua do Berço (to the left of a hotel called Estalagem de Monsaraz).

Go right after 250m at the second fork (ignore a small left turn), which is the less steeply downhill of the two, and follow this lovely cobbled road for 650 metres

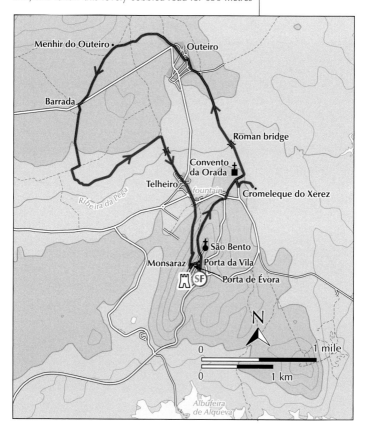

to a roundabout. Take the second exit anti-clockwise (signposted Cromoleque), then immediately turn left and walk along another cobbled road (Rua do Convento) for 300 metres, leading to **Convento da Orada**.

From the large paved area in front of the 18th-century convent, turn right along a cobbled road. Ignore the red/yellow cross (this is a 350-metre non-waymarked diversion) and then turn left, almost doubling back. Next, take a footpath on the right leading to a raised concrete walkway, and follow it to its end to the stone circle of **Cromeleque do Xerez**.

ALBUFEIRA DE ALQUEVA

The 250 sq km Albufeira is the result of the Alqueva Dam constructed in 2002 along Rio Guadiana, creating the largest artificial lake in Europe. Fields of olive, cork and holm oaks were submersed in the process.

The Cromeleque, a 5000-year-old megalithic monument, is a stone circle of 55 granitic blocks and was possibly related to fertility rituals. It was moved here to prevent it from being drowned by the rising lake waters.

This area is also famous as the first Starlight Tourist Destination certified by UNESCO.

After exploration, return to the convent and turn right, heading north-east, keeping the convent to the left. As the road curves left, take the footpath that's to the left of the road. Cross a beautiful **Roman bridge** over Ribeira da Pêga, reach a tarmac road and turn left and uphill. Continue straight on for just over 1km, ignoring a right-hand fork, to reach the village of **Outeiro**.

Opposite house number 10, take a right-hand turn onto a cobbled road (Rua da Esperança), and then take the first left on a cobbled road (Travessa da Padaria) to a square called Largo de Nossa Senhora da Orada. At the front of the Centro Culturo de Outeiro, go right along Rua da Alegria.

After 250 metres, at the end of this road, turn left then immediately right along Rua do Norte. Then go left at the next two forks, walking on dirt roads. At a crossroads 700

metres after Rua do Norte, go straight ahead, leading in 250 metres to **Menhir do Outeiro**.

> At 5.6m in height, this is the largest **menhir** (standing stone) in Portugal. Discovered only in 1964, it was re-erected in situ in 1969. It is thought to have been the focus of phallic worship, with carvings representing the glans and urethra.

Soon go left at a fork, leading to the hamlet of **Barrada** in 750 metres. Walk past a church on the left and reach a tarmac road. Turn right then immediately left. Stay on this road to the end of the town, then go straight ahead at a crossroads onto a dirt road, heading south. This leads to a T-junction next to the hotel; turn right, heading west, and then take the first left.

After 500 metres go straight ahead when the main dirt track turns right. Turn right at the third crossroads 1km later (having gone straight over two previous crossroads). Cross over a **bridge** and after 300 metres arrive in **Telheiro**.

Continue straight on, ignoring all turnings and heading towards Monsaraz. Just past the **fountain** by the police station (Guarda Nacional Republicana; GNR), go straight ahead where the main road turns left, with a primary school on the right. Reach a crossroads and

The flooded landscape of Albufeira de Alqueva, viewed from the tower of Monsaraz Castle

A beautiful stone path and wall in Monsaraz

Porta de Évora used to be the main entrance into Monsaraz, at the end of the Roman road.

continue straight ahead. Zigzag up, following waymarks, to arrive at a gate called **Porta de Évora**. ◄

Turn acutely left and walk along the course of the walls to **Porta da Vila** with a white square clocktower. Go through the gate, turn right, then go past a car park on the left and reach a roundabout. Turn left and arrive back at the start in **Monsaraz**.

SOUTHERN PORTUGAL

The wetlands of Ribeira de Seixe, leading to the beach and the Atlantic Ocean (Walk 34)

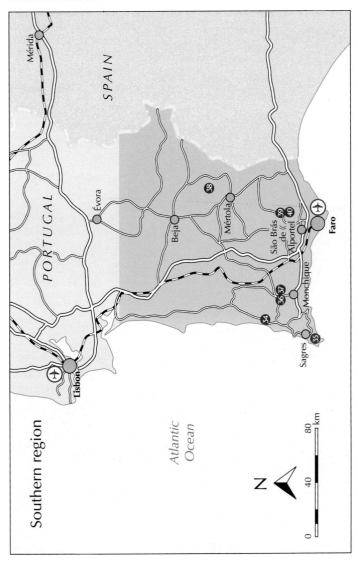

Southern region

THE ALGARVE, COSTA VICENTINA AND GUADIANA

Stunning cliff views and the pristine Praia das Adegas. Praia de Odeceixe (Walk 34) is just visible

The Algarve is perhaps best known for its holiday resorts, and while there is an undeniably touristy element to the area, most of the walks in this section are surrounded by nothing but nature and solitude, with the occasional foray into almost deserted villages.

The region has two mountain ranges – Serra de Monchique and Serra da Caldeirão – the latter translating as 'cauldron'; even in April it can feel hot enough to cook food on the ground. It is therefore best avoided in summer, although some years even October is too hot for comfortable walking. Undoubtedly the best time to visit is spring, when you will be surrounded by a profusion of wildflowers. If bird-life is of more interest you might want to visit in autumn for the annual migration of millions of birds.

Winter walking is possible, but even though the Algarve boasts 300 days of sunshine a year, that leaves more than two months of rain, so be prepared to get wet (especially on walks that involve river crossings). However, this is more than compensated for by the sight of countless almond trees turning the hillsides white with their blossom (mid January to mid February).

The Southwest Alentejo and Costa Vicentina Nature Park is a narrow

Walking by the levada (Walk 34)

coastal strip 110km long, leading from rural Alentejo to the south-western-most point of continental Europe, via the only untamed stretch of the Algarve coastline. It provides stunning clifftop walks with unique habitats for plants and animals, and the cooling Atlantic winds make summer walking possible, with beaches never far away.

The Guadiana Valley Nature Park is in the south-eastern extremity of Alentejo, bordering the Algarve. Mértola is a well-preserved walled town, perched on a peninsula between the Rio Guadiana and Ribeira Oeiras; it was settled by the Phoenicians, and was a very important Roman town before being conquered by the Moors and finally reconquered by the Order of Santiago (a rebranded Knights Templar). Creatures specific to this area are bustards, lesser kestrels and lynx.

BASES

The Algarve is a vast area. On its western side, accommodation is available at Odeceixe village, the beginning of Walk 34. For Walks 35, and 36/37, ample facilities are available at the nearby towns of Sagres and Monchique respectively. The best base for Walk 38 is the beautiful historic walled town of Mértola. Walk 40 is on the eastern side of the Algarve, where the coastal holiday town Faro (with an airport) or the quieter town of São Brás de Alportel would make convenient bases.

WALK 34
Odeceixe beach circuit

Start/Finish	Beside the seating area/café at Odeceixe beach (N37°26.445' W08°47.892')
Distance	13km
Total ascent	350m
Grade	Medium
Time	4hrs
Terrain	Some tarmac road, followed by footpath next to a *levada* (water channel), ending with an excellent clifftop stretch
Map	Carta Militar 1:50,000 sheet 49-4, 1:25,000 sheets 568 and 576
Refreshments	At start (seasonal only) and in Odeceixe
Toilets	At start and on map
Access	On the N120 between Odemira and Aljezur, just to the south of the Ribeira de Seixe is a westward turning signposted Praia de Odeceixe. Follow signs to the beach and restaurants.
Parking	At start

This is part of the Rota Vicentina Fisherman's Trail, waymarked blue/green, slightly altered to finish with a delightful stroll along a *levada* and a stunning clifftop footpath, resplendent with wildflowers in spring, sea birds all around and white storks nesting on clifftops. The route also includes part of Portugal's GR11 (waymarked red/white).

The **Ribeira de Seixe** runs from Monchique to the coast and enters the sea at Odeceixe beach. Along the way, it leaves sediments on its bank, creating natural wetland habitats. The beautiful golden sandy beach with its relaxed atmosphere provides a perfect location for a break.

The initial part of the route is parallel to Ribeira de Seixe all the way to Odeceixe, providing a good landmark and vista.

▶ Begin by heading south-east uphill, walk along the tarmac road Estrada da Praia de Odeceixe for 2km, and

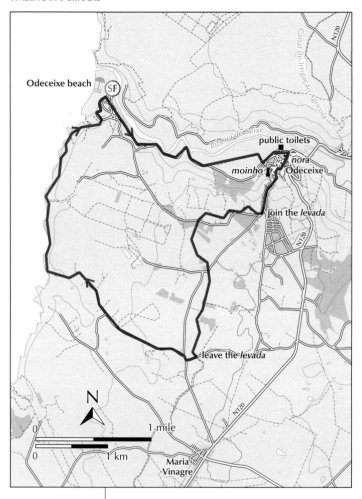

then take the only left-hand turn (just after a restaurant on the right). Follow this dirt road for 800 metres to its end, arrive back on the tarmac road and turn left, heading north-east.

After 100 metres reach a fork and go left on the out-skirts of Odeceixe (no waymarkings at all in town). Keep to the left, then there's a **public toilet** on the left, and take the first right after a *nora*.

Ribeira de Seixe with Odeceixe nestled in the valley

A *nora* is a donkey-powered system for raising water to a storage tank for the irrigation system. Buckets are raised on a giant bicycle chain and emptied into the channel.

▸ Walk along this road, Rua do Rio, and reach Largo 1° Maio with a fountain. At the top of the square turn left into Rua Nova, then take the first right, a pedes-trian street called Rua do Outão. At the end of the street turn right into Rua 25 de Abril, followed by a right turn just after a church to head up some steps. Turn right at the top, along Rua das Camélias, and then left at the end of the road, aiming towards a *moinho* (windmill).

There's a big sign for Rota Vicentina and this is also the official beginning of this section of GR11.

Walk up the steep road, past the **moinho** on the right, and up the hill. At a fork, go right along Rua da Charneca, then turn right at the **levada**, following GR11. Walk along the right-hand side of the *levada* ignoring any turnings

217

until it reaches a road bridge. Cross the bridge and walk on the left side of the *levada*.

In less than 300 metres the beautiful footpath becomes a dirt road. After a further 100m the dirt road crosses the *levada*; immediately after that, turn left and walk along the right side of the *levada*. Cross over two tarmac and two dirt roads, arrive at a T-junction with a tarmac road (about 3km from the start of *levada*), turn right and **leave the *levada***.

At the end of the road, turn right and then first left to go along a pretty and incredibly quiet tarmac road. Reach a dead-end after 2km and take the right-hand footpath. This immediately forks but both options lead to the same place.

The next 2.75km is along a beautiful, easy-to-follow section of clifftop footpath, sometimes on sand, with a plethora of wildflowers. It goes over a stream and bridge, then reaches a tarmac road at the end of the cliff path. Turn left towards **Odeceixe beach** and the start.

WALK 35
Cabo de São Vicente

Start/Finish	The lighthouse, Cabo de São Vicente (Cape Vincent) (N37°01.384′ W08°59.740′)
Distance	14.5km
Total ascent	310m
Grade	Medium
Time	4½hrs
Terrain	Starts on attractive but uneven coastal footpath; some dirt road and tarmac
Map	Carta Militar 1:50,000 sheet 51-1, 1:25,000 sheets 601 and 609
Refreshments	Restaurant (marked on map, seasonal opening) and there may be mobile snack bars near start
Access	From Sagres follow the N268 as far west as possible
Parking	At start

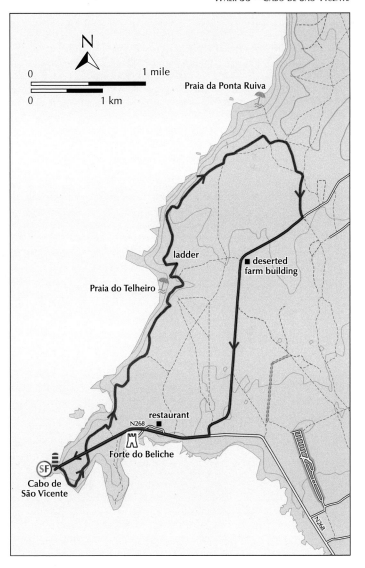

This is a magical walk along the cliff edge heading north along the Rota Vicentina Fisherman's Trail. To make it circular, it returns via the very ends of GR11, Rota Vicentina Historical Trail and GR13 Via Algarviana (this last section is also an *EcoVia* – a multipurpose route used by walkers and cyclists). Prepare to be delighted by the greenery and wildflowers in spring, a very unusual subset of vegetation (dwarfed low-lying plants), and above all, views of cliffs and the crashing surf of the Atlantic Ocean.

Rota Vicentina is the newest long-distance route in Portugal. Some 230km in length, its Historical section includes old ways that the locals, pilgrims and merchants used to travel between towns and villages, whereas the routes of its Fisherman's Trail were used for fishing.

This section is an official path but is not waymarked.

Walk away from the lighthouse and take the very first right-hand footpath to explore the cliffs. ◄ Follow the cliff edge to the end of the promontory, with a view of stark cliffs plus a huge deep sea cave, and then head north, inland.

Reach a tarmac road (**N268**) after 500 metres and go straight across it, now following the red/white waymarking of Via Algarviana. Go right at the next fork, and after the path curves right, immediately take a very indistinct footpath on the left, heading north and following the faint green/blue waymarking of the Fisherman's Trail on low stones. (If this turning is missed you'll come to a tarmac road in 150 metres; retrace steps from there.)

This follows the coastline and the terrain is stony and uneven. About 900m after the last turn, the path curves inland to a crossroads; go straight across, now heading back towards the sea. At the next fork go left and follow the coastline again for 850 metres. Take a big left-hand turn, which leads to the cliffs above **Praia do Telheiro**.

Continue for 400 metres to a *barranco* (ravine) and go down then back up again to a car parking area. Go straight across to a path, heading towards the sea.

Halfway down this wide dead-end path, take a footpath on the right, signposted with green arrows. At a footpath crossroads a minute later, go right for 200 metres then go down another *barranco* and up again via a **ladder**.

Just after the ladder, follow the main path forking right and uphill to the top of the *barranco*. The footpath then becomes a cart track; follow it along the coastline for nearly 2km, heading north. Arrive at a T-junction and go left, and follow the main path to another T-junction. Go right, heading away from the sea. ▶ Arrive at a three-way junction after 350 metres and go right along GR11, heading south. (The left-hand path is also GR11 but to Vila de Bispo.)

After 500 metres arrive at a T-junction with another dirt road and turn left. (There might be a pile of earth here – an anti-vehicle measure.) A dirt track then joins the route from the left, immediately followed by a fork where the route goes right. This leads to a T-junction with a very big dirt road; turn right, still following GR11.

Stay on the main track for 1km, and it becomes tarmac at a **deserted farm building**. Walk along for a

Praia do Telheiro, with the lighthouse of the cape in the distance

There's a left-hand turning going to a good beach, Praia da Ponta Ruiva.

221

further 2.5km, keeping an eye out for little bustards, to a T-junction with a tarmac road (**N268**). Turn right and walk along the *EcoVia*, a bit of hardcore just to the left of the tarmac road. After 800 metres go past a **restaurant**, then **Forte do Beliche** 200 metres later. Carry on for about 1.5km to return to the start at the **lighthouse** on Cabo de São Vicente (Cape Vincent).

CAPE VINCENT

Cape Vincent is the most south-westerly tip of Europe and a birdwatchers' favourite. The lighthouse is built over a monastery, the destination of the St Vincent pilgrimage, hence the end of Rota Vicentina. He was a fourth-century martyred Iberian deacon who was brought ashore and buried here. The shrine was allegedly guarded by ravens and they accompanied the relics when they were exhumed and transported to Lisbon, as depicted in Lisbon's coat of arms.

WALK 36

*Rota das Cascatas,
Monchique*

Start/Finish	Fóia summit, Monchique (N37°18.934' W08°35.521')
Distance	18.5km
Total ascent	1100m
Grade	Challenging
Time	7½hrs
Terrain	Footpaths, dirt roads, and a small amount on very quiet tarmac
Map	Carta Militar 1:50,000 sheets 49-3 and 49-4, 1:25,000 sheets 577 and 585
Refreshments	At start
Toilets	At start
Access	From Monchique follow the N266-3 to the summit of Fóia
Parking	At start

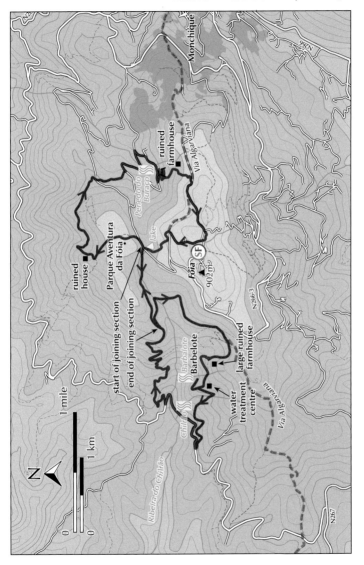

Rain or shine, PR5 Rota das Cascatas ('route of the waterfalls') is a delight. It takes in the highest mountain in the Algarve (Fóia, 902m; adorned with the usual aerial masts) and impressive views, plenty of ruined farms/villages, spectacular terracing, and the highest portion of GR13 Via Algarviana. Despite the fact that it looks a funny shape on the map (two circular walks with a joining section), this is an official waymarked route.

The best times for this walk are in late spring for the rare Iberian peonies, just after heavy rains for the spectacular waterfalls, and on a clear day for the views.

The route goes past three cascades: Barbelote is the most beautiful and imposing of the three in a stunning location, next to the ancient village of the same name; Chilrão waterfall forms the head of Ribeira da Cerca which flows all the way to the coast in Aljezur, and Penedo do Buraco is a seasonal waterfall in an inaccessible cliff.

Fóia in Serra da Monchique is at 902m the highest point in Algarve. From here on a good day you can see as far as the coastline. There's a plaque at the summit telling the story of Captain Pedro da Silva who spotted the greenery of Fóia from the sea and thus managed to save his ship from a bad storm. In gratitude, he built a convent below the summit.

The walk begins from a noticeboard south-east of the café at the summit. From there, head north on a tarmac road following the red/yellow waymarked PR5. ◄ When the road curves left, take a footpath at the bend on the right, then fork left immediately and go through a vertical swing gate.

Be careful not to follow red/yellow waymarking of PR3.

Walk along, keeping the pond to your left, then veer right and away from the tarmac road, following red/white/yellow waymarking. Arrive at a cart track after 150 metres, turn left and then immediately right onto a footpath. Walk past a small **lake** and through another gate to a tarmac road.

This next part is the joining section, which is just over 1km and will be walked in both directions.

◄ Go straight ahead onto a dirt road, following red/white/yellow waymarking. Continue to a T-junction with a dilapidated building and go left, heading north-east and following signs for PR5 and GR13.

The route passes some ruined farm buildings and very neat terracing, now used for grazing only. Follow the main path for 1.5km to a fork and go right, which is level (not the uphill option). At the next fork, go right and downhill (GR13 Via Algarviana forks left). Arrive at a crossroads 300 metres later, go straight ahead, and then 150 metres after a **large ruined farmhouse**, take an indistinct but lovely right-hand footpath going steeply down. ▶

At this point the cart track is a lot wider and the ruined village of Barbelote is visible to the right.

Fork left at the bottom of the footpath (right leads to Barbelote) and continue for 200 metres until arriving back at the cart track, then turn right and head downhill. Just after a **water treatment centre** the cart track turns acutely left; take the right-hand path here, signposted 'Cascata do Barbelote 250m', to a viewpoint with a lovely polished granite seat. Afterwards retrace steps back to the cart track and turn right.

Follow the cart track downhill for about 250 metres and take an easily missed right-hand rough cart track, just before a ravine. This runs on the right-hand side of

Neat terracing and old farmhouses in the ruined village of Barbelote. The view stretches all the way to both coastlines of the Algarve

the ravine and joins a main cart track heading downhill. Arrive at a fork 800 metres later and go right, immediately followed by another fork where you go right. About 100 metres later, at a T-junction with a tarmac road, turn right, heading east.

Walk past **Cascata do Chilrão** and take the first right-hand turn; a cart track zigzagging steeply uphill. After 500 metres continue straight ahead onto a lesser-used cart track (ignoring the main track going left). The route then becomes a good footpath through the trees, and zigzags uphill for 650 metres to a T-junction with a cart track. Turn right and zigzag uphill again for another kilometre, heading back to the joining section.

Penedo do Buraco waterfall

Walk along the joining section back to the tarmac road and the **lake** and turn left. After 150 metres take the first left, a cart track signposted 'Parque Aventura da Fóia'. Stay on the main cart track to go past the **adventure park** – ignoring the official route which veers unnecessarily right then back to the cart track – and at the top of the track go straight ahead along a lesser-used cart track.

Continue downhill, ignoring any turnings, past a stone-built **ruined house** (about 700 metres from the park), and then descend passing some terracing. Go straight ahead on the main path to a T-junction with another dirt road and turn right. Take the second left, which leads to a T-junction with a tarmac road after 500 metres, then turn left and downhill. Walk 350 metres along the tarmac to another waterfall, **Cascata do Penedo do Buraco**.

After 250 metres take the first right-hand tarmac road uphill, signposted as a dead-end. After 600 metres take the second left turn, through a gate that is there to stop cars and not people. Just 100 meters along here is a **picnic area** plus a drinking water tap, shortly before a building where the tarmac ends and the route becomes a cart track. Turn immediate right after the building and walk up the steeply ascending footpath through terracing, then along one of the terraces. This becomes a dirt road leading to a crossroads 200 metres after the building; turn acutely left heading south-east and uphill, along a very rough cart track.

After 100 metres take an indistinct and poorly way-marked left-hand turn to a narrow footpath. This path zig-zags up for 500 metres along a cart track and eventually past an old **ruined farmhouse** with terracing, to a tarmac road. (If the indistinct turning is missed, just battle on, heading upwards and south to the tarmac road.) At the road turn right and follow PR3 and PR5 towards the host of aerials visible at **Fóia summit**. ▶ Make your way back to the start.

Ignore GR13 which veers off to the right.

WALK 37
Trilho da Fóia, Monchique

Start/Finish	Fóia summit, Serra de Monchique (N37°18.934′ W08°35.521′)
Alternative start	N266-3 road 3.3km from Monchique towards Fóia summit (N37°18.449′ W08°35.109′)
Distance	7km
Total ascent	360m
Grade	Easy
Time	2½hrs
Terrain	Footpaths, dirt road, and a small amount of tarmac
Map	Carta Militar 1:50,000 sheet 49-3, 1:25,000 sheet 585
Refreshments	At start and at alternative start
Toilets	At start
Access	From Monchique follow the N266-3 to Fóia summit
Parking	At start

For a short walk, PR3 (waymarked in red/yellow) certainly packs in a lot. Beginning from the highest point in the Algarve – Fóia summit (902m), where the superb views are not affected by the somewhat ugly buildings and aerials – it soon leaves the hordes of tourists behind to wander along quiet paths, past ancient farms and terracing. The lower alternative start is useful if high temperatures are predicted, as this gets the steep ascent out of the way early in the day (and finishes at a restaurant for lunch).

> **Serra de Monchique** is ideal for agricultural purposes, with a mild Mediterranean climate and rain clouds from the Atlantic. The solution to the steep hillside terrain was to create terracing, maximising the area for planting, preventing erosion and reducing surface runoff. Used since Moorish times for planting crops, most terraces are now left fallow or only used for grazing due to years of agricultural decline.

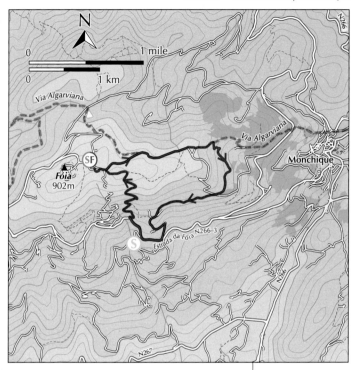

The walk begins from a noticeboard south-east of the café at the summit. From there, head south along a path to a little aggregation of naked rock. Curve left for 50 metres and arrive at a tarmac road. Turn right, and then go left at a fork. Continue on PR3, soon joined by the red/white waymarked GR13 (Via Algarviana). ▶ After being on the tarmac road for 1.3km, when the main tarmac road curves right, go left onto a rough cart track waymarked white/red/yellow.

Descend to a T-junction with a less rough dirt road and turn left, heading downhill. After 250 metres turn right (GR13 goes straight ahead), and shortly afterwards is a crossroads; turn left along a lovely footpath. This

Be careful not to take a footpath on the left, which is PR5, also waymarked red/yellow.

Beautiful terracing in Serra de Monchique in a veil of fog

merges with another cart track and then arrives at a cross-roads; go straight ahead over the tarmac road. Turn right at a T-junction 1km further on and go downhill for 600 metres to the tarmac road **N266-3**, then turn right and uphill.

Along this tarmac road is the **alternative start** with two restaurants (Restaurante Rampa and Paraiso da Montanha). About 400 metres after the restaurants, go up the second turning on the right. ◀ Follow the cobbled road, which zigzags steeply up for 1.5km. The route becomes a cart track, leading to one of the aerial collections and then to the tarmac road at the beginning. Retrace steps to the start on **Fóia**.

Ignore the sign that says private property – this is for cars, not walkers.

WALK 38
Pulo do Lobo, Guadiana

Start/Finish	Signboard (see access), Guadiana Valley Nature Park (N37°48.899', W07°38.977')
Distance	5.5km
Total ascent	250m
Grade	Easy
Time	3hrs
Terrain	Uneven rocky path along the riverbank; dirt track and small amount of tarmac
Map	Carta Militar 1:50,000 sheet 46-1, 1:25,000 sheet 541
Access	From Mértola, go north along the N122 towards Beja, turning right at about 3km, signposted for Corte de Gafo de Cima. Then follow the road signs for Pulo do Lobo to the start (the signboard is on the left 200 metres before a gate at the end of the road).
Parking	At start (space for two cars only; if full there is more space along the tarmac road)

Pulo do Lobo ('wolf's leap') refers to the waterfall running between the organically sculpted weathered rocks in the heart of Guadiana valley, formed about 100,000 years ago. The waymarked PR9 may sound easy but there's a brilliantly untamed section along the river, with the path indistinct in places and very uneven underfoot, making it more challenging. In return it offers phenomenal views of Rio Guadiana, frequented by Mediterranean turtles, plus a chance of seeing black storks and little bustards.

Start by walking south-east along the tarmac road for 700 metres. This ends at a **gate for Herdade de Pulo do Lobo**, where there's a sign in Portuguese meaning 'please go through and close the gate'. Go through it and follow the main dirt road downwards for 1.5km. There's a **picnic area** at the end of the road, and it's worth diverting to the right along a concrete walkway to some excellent views of the **falls** and the *marmitas de gigante* – huge rock cavities scoured by glacial water.

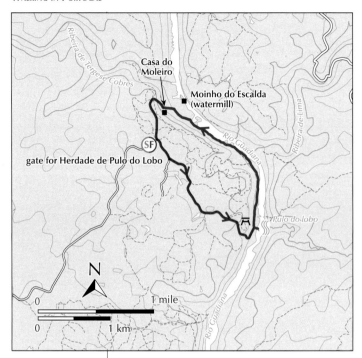

Casa do Moleiro

Moinho do Escalda (watermill)

SF

gate for Herdade de Pulo do Lobo

Rio Guadiana

Ribeira de Telgese-Cobres

Ribeira-de-Lima

Pulo do lobo

N

0   1 mile

0   1 km

Rio Guadiana

Legend has it that a poor peasant boy fell in love with a princess, regularly leaping across the waterfall to meet her. In an attempt to stop the relationship, the king cursed the boy and turned him into a wolf, but the lovers continued to meet. When the king tried to kill the boy, the lovers fled, leaping together over the falls. Unfortunately the princess fell into the torrent and perished, and in despair the boy/wolf followed her.

The route continues straight ahead along a lovely footpath, following the banks upstream. (The path is indistinct in places; if not clearly visible, just keep going upstream.) Just over 2km from the picnic area, turn left to

*Pulo do Lobo chasm,
surrounded by
intricately weathered
rock and marmitas
de gigante*

follow an easily missed path (look out for a ruined building on this side of the river – Moinho do Escalda).

Ascend for 150 metres and go past the ruined miller's
house (**Casa do Moleiro**), after which the path becomes a
cart track. Continue for 250 metres up to a T-junction with
another cart track and go left and uphill for 600 metres,
heading south. This leads to the tarmac road at the start.

WALK 39

GR23

Start/Finish	Roundabout in Cachopo (N37°20.037′ W07°49.038′)
Distance	46km
Total ascent	1550m
Grade	Easy (over 4 days) or challenging (over 2 days)
Time	16hrs (over 2–4 days)
Terrain	All on dirt road or cart track
Map	Carta Militar 1:50,000 sheets 50-3 and 50-4, 1:25,000 sheets 581 and 589
Refreshments	Cachopo only
Toilets	Cachopo (see route description)
Access	Cachopo is on the N124, 36km north of São Brás de Alportel
Parking	At start
Warning	River/stream crossings may be difficult after heavy rain

This excellent *grande rota* (waymarked red/white) could be done in 2 days (strenuously) or spread out longer (more leisurely), and it includes a section of GR13 Via Algarviana. It is far from the crowds, but also a long way from facilities and supplies. In spring the wildflowers blanket the hillsides and the water valleys are full of birdsong. Throughout the year on the hills there are tremendous views and absolute solitude.

SPLITTING THE ROUTE

To help you choose the level of the challenge, the broken-down figures are as follows:

Cachopo to Feiteira 14km, 610m ascent, 5hrs

Feiteira to Mealha 15km, 400m ascent, 5hrs

Mealha to Casas Baixas 13km, 420m ascent, 4½hrs

Casas Baixas to Cachopo 4km, 120m ascent, 1½hrs.

There is accommodation available in Centros de Descoberta do Mundo Rural (Rural World Discovery Centres) in Feiteira, Mealha and Casas Baixas, and rooms available in private houses in Cachopo. Prior booking required via ruralgarve.in-loco.pt or moinhocachopo@yahoo.com.br, tel +351 289 840 860 (office) or +351 964 784 685/+351 961 478 155 (local host phones). No English spoken, therefore it is probably easiest to email in Portuguese (use an online translator). Cooking facilities are available, or the local host can either cook for you or collect a take-away from one of the restaurants in Cachopo.

There are many turnings off the main route; they will not be mentioned in the route description, so ignore them unless instructed otherwise.

◀ From the start, head south-west following road signs for Fonte Férrea and Parque de Lazer, then take the very first left-hand turn which is Rua 1° de Maio. Then take the first left, reach the church (toilets underneath on the right), walk to its right and then turn right onto Rua da Igreja. At the end of the road turn right onto a little footpath which goes down to a cobbled road leading to a tarmac road, and turn left (ignore some erroneous waymarking). Go across a bridge 100 metres further on and then take the first left, following signs for GR13 and GR23 to Feiteira.

Redundant village primary schools are now rural tourist accommodation called Discovery Centres, testimony to the aging **population** in the depths of rural Algarve. Feiteira had 120 inhabitants in the 1960s; less than half remain and all of them are in their 60s, as are the remaining 20 residents of Casas Baixas. Mealha used to have 150 inhabitants in the 1950s; by 2000 there were 60. These are typical examples of the state of rural villages in Portugal, with many facing abandonment within the next few decades.

Follow this steep uphill cart track for 1km and arrive at a fork. Go left, followed immediately by another fork, and go left again (uphill) to go past a **ruined windmill**. The path then curves right, leading to a hamlet called **Currais**. Go through the village to a T-junction at the end, and turn right onto a tarmac road.

Take the first left-hand fork on the outskirts of the village, heading towards a water pump. Walk uphill along a crushed stone path which becomes a dirt road, to the top of a rise. Go straight ahead at a crossroads and follow road signs for Alcaria Alta. Continue on the main path for 1.7km and go past a **fort-like villa**.

After 2km reach a complicated junction (ignore two left-hand and one right-hand turns) and go straight ahead for 1km, then go right at a fork (left is signposted for Alcaria Alta). Reach a T-junction after 200 metres and turn right, following a road sign for Feiteira. This leads to a crossroads; go straight ahead for 900 metres, following GR13 towards Feiteira. ▶ At the next T-junction, turn left (right is a road signposted for 'Barragem'), and then at the following T-junction 700 metres later, turn left again, still following signs for Feiteira.

GR13 to Castelao and Barranco do Velho goes left.

After 850 metres, at a crossroads, go straight ahead (PR6 goes right, with red/yellow waymarkings). After a further 700 metres there are two turnings at the same place on the right-hand side, below some wind turbines; take the signposted second one, a rarely used cart track heading south-west. Continue on this cart track for just

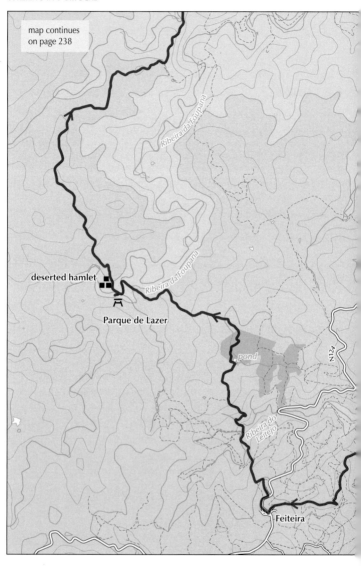

map continues
on page 238

Ribeira da Foupana

Ribeira da Foupana

deserted hamlet

Parque de Lazer

Ribeira da Foupana

pond

N124

Ribeira do Leitejo

Feiteira

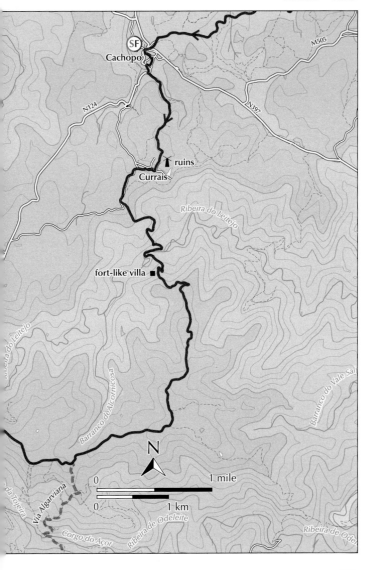

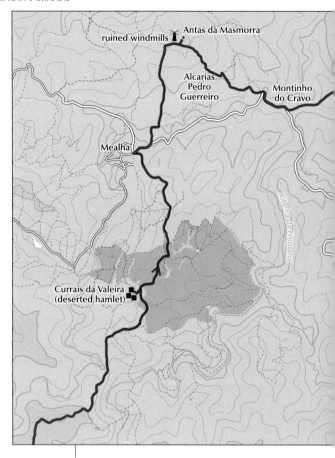

over 1km, going past a hairpin loop to the outskirts of **Feiteira**.

In the village, follow the concrete road to the main tarmac road and turn right. Walk along for 300 metres and take the fourth left-hand turning, onto a concrete path going upwards. This becomes a dirt road ending in a T-junction after 200 metres; go left. At the next T-junction,

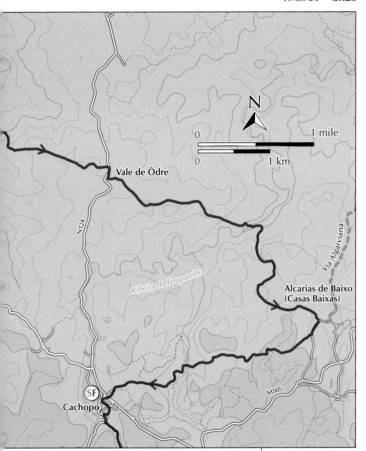

150 metres later, go right to reach a three-way junction. Go left, ignoring the red/yellow cross.

Ford **Ribeira do Leitejo**, and then the main path zig-zags up followed by a downward section. When it starts going up again, take a poorly signed left turn just before a **pond** (over 1km from the stream). Turn right after 50 metres, heading uphill. This soon leads to a T-junction;

Parque de Lazer picnic area can be reached by heading left and fording a river – usually very shallow but may be difficult after heavy rain.

turn left, now going downhill. After 350 metres take the first left-hand turning, with a road sign for Parque de Lazer (leisure park). Continue and then ford **Ribereira da Foupana**, after which the path goes straight up. ◄

Ascend and then go through a **deserted hamlet**, and then a beautiful valley. Arrive at a T-junction just over 1km after the hamlet and turn right. About 3.5km further on another path merges with the route and both go downhill.

Walk along a crest leading to a junction about 2km from the point where the paths merged. Two paths join from the left; take the first left of the two to the deserted village of **Currais da Valeira**, then retrace your steps back to the main route. Continue to follow the main path for 650 metres to reach a big T-junction, then turn left following road signs for Mealha. Just over 1.5km later, arrive at a tarmac road. To the left is the village of **Mealha** (there's a noticeboard with a map of the village). The route goes right, which is north-east.

Mealha has some **roundhouses**, of prehistoric origin, made of stones with cone-shaped thatched roofs of rushes from local streams. They were the living quarters of farmers (*casa circulares*) and later used as storage barns.

Take the first left-hand turn from the tarmac road after 300 metres – a dirt road heading downhill. Then cross a river on stepping-stones with a handrail (wire) after a further 300 metres, go left at the next fork and left again at the following fork. Continue for 900 metres to a T-junction with **ruined windmills** on the brow of the closest hill; turn right. At the windmills carry on straight ahead (ignore red/yellow and erroneous red/white way-markings on the right) and just after them, 70m to the left of the main trail, is the Neolithic **Antas da Masmorra**.

This 4000–5000-year-old megalithic funereal **monument**, circular in shape and surrounded by a 26m-diameter tumulus, is positioned on high ground, possibly as a territorial marker.

River-crossing using stepping-stones and a handrail

Continue on the main route, and just before some houses (**Alcarias Pedro Guerreiro**), fork left onto a lesser-used cart track. After 150 metres curve left then right (ignore a turning to the left on the bend), now heading south-east. Cross over a river on stepping-stones (with hand rail) 700 metres later and immediately turn left at a tarmac road. Ignore a turning on the left for the village of **Montinho do Cravo**, and 450 metres along the tarmac, take a left-hand dirt road going uphill, signposted Casas Baixas.

As you ascend there are some confusing waymarkings suggesting that there should be a turn, but just go straight ahead, admiring the pines planted along the contour lines. ▸ After 1km turn right on a lesser-used cart track heading south-east to **Ribeira da Foupana** (you'd arrive at a part of the river with nowhere to cross if this turning is missed).

After 150 metres, ford the river (which is usually very shallow) and go straight ahead, heading south on an indistinct cart track (ignore the big cart track on the left). Continue heading south, walking to the right of a *barranco* (ravine) filled with beautiful trees and wildflowers,

These are stone pine, planted as an anti-erosion measure with EU funding. From above they make beautiful, almost organic curving patterns.

Rolling hills planted with pines by the EU to prevent erosion, with rock roses in the foreground

and at the top of the rise the path turns 90° left. Cross over a gate then walk uphill, heading east.

At the very first building, 1km later, curve left along a dirt road (to the right is a gate; no waymarking here). Follow this for 400 metres to a tarmac road **N124** and turn right, keeping the main part of the village (**Vale de Ôdre**) to the left. After 50 metres, just by the last building of the village, in a sort of layby, turn left along a downward concrete track.

Take the first left after another 50 metres (straight ahead is a water hand pump with drinkable water), and then take the first right turn onto a cart track (just before the path leads back into the village). Continue for 600 metres to a T-junction with a more main dirt road and turn left, then immediately fork left. Go right at a fork 300 metres later, walking through very neatly terraced pines, and at the next fork go right again which is downhill leading to **Ribeira da Foupanilha**.

Ahead is Casas Baixas with a noticeboard displaying a map of the village.

Ford the river (usually very shallow) and follow the main track as it heads east initially. At a fork 1km later, go left and uphill with only red/yellow waymarking of PR2. Arrive at a tarmac road after a further 1.3km. ◀ Turn

242

right, which is also Via Algarviana. Take a right-hand turn 200 metres later onto a dirt road.

Go straight over the next crossroads, and 600 metres later arrive at a five-way junction (ignore two right options and one left). Go straight ahead, and then cross another river with stepping-stones and immediately come to a T-junction. Go left, leading to another five-way junction about 1km later (ignore two right options and one ahead). The route goes left and leads to a tarmac road after 200 metres; turn right and follow the road back to **Cachopo** and the start.

On the trail, walking through very neatly terraced pines

WALK 40
Serra do Caldeirão, Parizes

Start/Finish	Bus stop in Parizes (N37°14.866' W07°51.161')
Distance	20km
Total ascent	840m
Grade	Difficult
Time	7hrs
Terrain	Mostly dirt road
Map	Carta Militar 1:50,000 sheet 50-3, 1:25,000 sheets 589 and 598
Refreshments	Café at start
Access	From São Brás de Alportel, take the N2 north for about 3km to the village of Alportel, where there's a road forking right onto M1202, signed Parizes (also spelled Parises).
Parking	On road between the bus stop and the church
Warning	River/stream crossings may be difficult after heavy rain

The full name of this walk is PR2 'Entre vales, fontes e memórias da Serra do Caldeirão' – 'Among valleys, springs and memories of the Cauldron Mountains'. It is an unusual PR walk (waymarked red/yellow), in that it's a good length with significant total ascent.

A hugely enjoyable walk with long crest sections and excellent views, the horizons seem bigger and more open here compared to elsewhere in the Algarve. In spring when the countryside is lush green and bright with wildflowers, the brooks are burbling gently, the birds fill the skies with their song and the frogs do the same in the valleys, you might ask yourself how this place has remained such a well-kept secret. (But don't ask too loudly...)

TO BREAK THIS WALK INTO TWO

This walk comprises two main loops forming a figure of 8, plus a shorter loop. The main loops can be walked independently to create two shorter walks.

First loop (10km, 460m ascent, 3½hrs)

Starting from Parizes, follow the main route until you reach the **big junction** of Ribeira das Ruivas and Ribeira da Ameixeira (where the two loops intersect), then take an acute left-hand turn just before the route crosses the river, onto a footpath not well signed heading north. Follow this to Várzea do Velho, then continue on the route back to Parizes.

Second loop (10km, 380m ascent, 3½hrs)

Start at the **road junction** near Barranco da Figueira (N37°14.540′ W07°49.787′). Follow the main route until you reach the **big junction** of Ribeira das Ruivas and Ribeira da Ameixeira (the intersection point of the two loops), then turn left and follow the earlier part of the route description from this junction back to your start point.

To get to the road junction (the start point for the second loop) by car

Continue along M1202 past Parizes for about 2km until there's a pair of ruined windmills on the left and a car park with a viewpoint on the right, then turn second right, along a downhill road signposted for Barranco da Figueira. After 400 metres, park near a multi-way junction.

From the start, walk south-west along the tarmac road, heading away from the church. Turn left just before a café/shop and then turn immediate right heading south on a dirt road, walking down the river valley. About 2km outside the village, take a left-hand turn (where there's a road sign for Javali straight ahead) onto a lesser-used cart track. After just 50 metres, ford **Ribeira das Ruivas**, go up the cart track and at the top of a rise turn acute left at a T-junction with a dirt road, heading east.

Go along this gorgeous crest walk for 1.5km, with views down to the valley in both directions, until the path starts to descend. Continue along the main path downhill (ignore a lesser-travelled fork to the right) to a big junction with a road sign for Várzea do Velho – a deserted village that's encountered later.

Go straight ahead, now also following GR13 Via Algarviana Ligação 1, waymarked red/white/yellow. (GR13 Link 1 goes from Parizes to São Brás de Alportel.) Reach the bottom of the hill at a crossroads 1.1km later

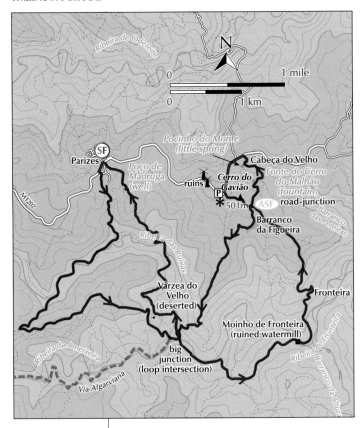

The two main loops of the walk intersect here.

and go straight ahead, heading east (GR13 goes right). Arrive at a **big junction**, where Ribeira das Ruivas meets Ribeira da Ameixeira and becomes Ribeira de Fronteira. ◀

The route continues on the main track, crossing **Ribeira da Ameixeira** via stepping-stones, heading south and then going up for 50 metres. Continue for 650 metres along the beautiful valley floor with the **Ribeira de Fronteira** on your left, and at a T-junction with a more main dirt road (with a road sign for Pero de Amigos), turn right. Go up the hill, straight over a crossroads at the top and then descend again.

Continue following the main path and ford several streams, including Ribeira de Fronteira at the ruined **Moinho de Fronteira** 1.5km from the last T-junction. Then go up the hill towards the small hamlet of Fronteira with the river in the valley on the right.

Arrive at **Fronteira**, from where there is hardly any waymarking until the next village. Follow the main road going upwards through the hamlet, and then continue along the main dirt road as it zigzags steeply upwards. (Along the way, look out for the traditional beehives made of cork.) Go straight ahead at the next crossroads, 1.3km after Fronteira, then down a little and the dirt road becomes tarmac. Arrive at a tarmac **road junction** 500 meters later. ▶

The second of the two main loops (see box) starts here.

Cork beehives are rarely seen anymore except in rural mountain villages in Portugal. They are made using ancient traditional methods dating back to Roman times. Cork is a light and versatile material with low heat conductivity, making it the perfect material for beehives as it keeps the bees inside cool.

Traditional beehives made from cork

The small loop above the multi-way junction, included here for its points of interest, is poorly way-marked, overgrown, difficult to follow and could be omitted (shortening the walk by 2km and ¾hr). However, to continue on it, take an indistinct right-hand footpath heading north-east, just before the first building of the village, walking to the right of a wall. This merges with another cart track from the right; go through a gap in the wall and head north-east, walking to the left of the wall, parallel to the cart track.

The route becomes a very infrequently used 'old way' between two walls. Follow it down as it curves left, heading west, and reach the well of **Fonte do Cerro do Malhão** 350 metres from the road junction. Follow the route north as it curves right along the valley to head east. ◄ When the double wall ends in 200 metres, turn left to follow a path between another pair of walls, heading north uphill. This path is particularly gorgeous, although there is no waymarking at all. Arrive at a little spring called **Pocinho do Monte** 350 metres later and turn right, going uphill.

Go through the village of **Cabeça do Velho** to a T-junction with a tarmac road and turn left uphill, ignoring red/yellow PR4 waymarking. Walk along the tarmac road, ignore a left turn and after 700 metres arrive at a junction with multiple options, with a bus stop on the right-hand side and a **car park with a viewpoint** in front. Take the first left-hand turn (the second left-hand turn has a sign for PR2 but this only goes to the football café), and go along a downhill road signposted for Barranco da Figueira for 400 metres, leading back to the tarmac **road junction**.

Turn right, following another road sign for Barranco da Figueira. At the end of the tarmac road, 400 metres later, take a footpath on the right-hand side. This descends then soon forks; go right. Arrive at a fork with a more major dirt road and go right, which is uphill. Reach a T-junction after 200 metres and go left, along a dirt road. Follow this for 1.3km, then on a downhill section take an acute right-hand turning off the main path, heading

The official path is between two walls, but if it's overgrown you can walk just above it on its right.

Impressive wildflower display in front of the deserted village of Várzea do Velho

west (the turning is opposite a gap between two sections of crash barrier on the left). After 500 metres, this leads to the **big junction** of Ribeira das Ruivas and Ribeira da Ameixeira. ▶

The two main loops of the walk intersect here.

Cross over **Ribeira das Ruivas** via stepping-stones and turn right, heading north, along a lovely little-used cart track along the river. After 350 metres, turn 90° left to walk steeply uphill along an indistinct footpath. Arrive at the deserted village of **Várzea do Velho** 200 metres later and turn right. Walk out of the village along a footpath for about 70 metres to reach a T-junction with a cart track; turn right and uphill, now also following Via Algarviana Ligação 1 (waymarked red/white/yellow).

After 1.3km, cross **Ribeira das Ruivas** again using stepping-stones hidden in the foliage on the left. Follow the path as it curves right after 100 metres, heading north and uphill. Stay on the main path for 1km until Parizes is visible across the valley. Turn left, then immediately right onto a footpath heading north.

After 300 metres, just when the route seems nearly at its end, there is one more descent and ascent, but on a terrific footpath. Walk past the well of **Poço de Madruga**

An amazingly neat pile of harvested cork in the village Parizes

then follow the stone-built Caminho do Vale da Cruz upwards, passing the **Parizes** *lavadouros* (communal washing area) to return to the start.

VEGETATION AND LAND USE

This area used to be covered with native cork and holm oak trees. Over the years, due to intensive farming (especially the 1930s Wheat Campaign) as well as pine and eucalyptus plantations, the natural vegetation and habitats have been significantly destroyed. The soil has become very poor and other plants – those that tolerate dry poor soil, like rock roses – have taken over, creating a different ecosystem. This has had a huge impact on mountain life; hunting, grazing animals, cork production and farming have become difficult and many villages have been deserted.

APPENDIX A
Route summary table

Walk	Name	Start	Type	Distance (km)	Ascent (m)	Grade	Time (hrs)	Page
Peneda-Gerês National Park								
1	Caminho dos Mortos	near Real	Circular	12.5	650	Medium	5	37
2	Trilho Castrejo	Castro Laboreiro	Circular	17	820	Difficult	6½	42
3	Peneda circuit	Peneda	Circular	24	1200	Challenging	9	48
4	Pertinho do Céu	Gavieira	Circular	8.5	600	Medium	3½	54
5	Bicos and Pedrada	Porta do Mezio	Circular	18 or 25	540 or 780	Difficult or challenging	6 or 8½	58
6	Pitões das Júnias	Pitões das Júnias	Circular	12.5 or 4.5 or 13.5	760 or 220 or 760	Medium or easy or difficult	5 or 1½ or 5½	63
7	Minas dos Carris	Portela de Homem	There-and-back	21	930	Difficult	7	68
8	Gerês circuit*	Campo do Gerês	Circular	25	1400	(Very) challenging	11	72
9	Água do Sarilhão and Via Nova	Campo do Gerês	Circular	16	650	Medium	5½	80
10	Trilho dos Currais	Vila do Gerês	Circular	10	680	Medium	4	85
Montesinho Nature Park								
11	Trilho da Calçada	Moimenta	Circular	8	350	Easy	3	92

Walk	Name	Start	Type	Distance (km)	Ascent (m)	Grade	Time (hrs)	Page
12	Montesinho summits	Montesinho	Circular	22.5 or 7	680 or 300	Difficult or easy	7½ or 2½	95
Around Alvão Nature Park								
13	Senhora da Graça	Mondim de Basto	Circular	14.5	850	Difficult	6	102
14	Marão summit	Soutelo	There-and-back	13	860	Difficult	5	106
Douro International Nature Park								
15	Azeite	Bruçó	There-and-back	8.5	440	Easy	3½	110
16	Ribeira do Mosteiro	Ribeira do Mosteiro	Circular	9	380	Easy	3½	112
Schist villages								
17	Schist villages of Lousã	Lousã	Circular	18.5	1400	Challenging	9	118
18	Caminho do Xisto das Aldeias de Góis and Lousã summit	Comareira	Circular	8.5 or 16	550 or 950	Medium or difficult	3½ or 6½	126
19	Trilho do Vale do Ceira	Cabreira	Circular	13	800	Medium	5½	131

Serra da Estrela Nature Park

APPENDIX A – ROUTE SUMMARY TABLE

Walk	Name	Start	Type	Distance (km)	Ascent (m)	Grade	Time (hrs)	Page
20	Sol and Rota das Faias	Manteigas	Circular	11	600	Medium	4½	138
21	Rota do Carvão	Manteigas	Circular	21	1150	Challenging	8	141
22	Javali and Poço do Inferno	Manteigas	Circular	14	1100	Difficult	6	148
23	Rota do Glaciar	Torre	Linear (finish: Manteigas)	18.5	210	Difficult	6½	152
24	Poios Brancos	Covão d'Ametade	Circular	8	330	Easy	3	158

Around Lisbon

Walk	Name	Start	Type	Distance (km)	Ascent (m)	Grade	Time (hrs)	Page
25	Castelejo	Alvados	Circular	13	410	Medium	4½	165
26	Chãos	Chãos	Circular	15	460	Medium	5	170
27	Peninha	Santuário da Peninha	Circular	5	175	Easy	2	175
28	Cabo Espichel	Cabo Espichel	Circular	10.5	450	Medium	4	178

Tejo and São Mamede Nature Parks

Walk	Name	Start	Type	Distance (km)	Ascent (m)	Grade	Time (hrs)	Page
29	Rota dos Abutres	Salvaterra do Extremo	Circular	11.5	275	Medium	4	184

Walk	Name	Start	Type	Distance (km)	Ascent (m)	Grade	Time (hrs)	Page
30	GR29 Rota dos Veados*	Rosmaninhal	Circular	41	1030	Challenging	13hrs (or 2 days)	188
31	Marvão	Portagem	Circular	8	390	Easy	3	197
Monsaraz and Évora								
32	Évora aqueduct and Ecopista	Évora	Circular	18.5	210	Medium	5	202
33	Monsaraz	Monsaraz	Circular	11	230	Easy	3½	206
The Algarve, Costa Vicentina and Guadiana								
34	Odeceixe beach circuit	Odeceixe beach	Circular	13	350	Medium	4	215
35	Cabo de São Vicente	Cabo de São Vicente lighthouse	Circular	14.5	310	Medium	4½	218
36	Rota das Cascatas	Monchique	Circular	18.5	1100	Challenging	7½	222
37	Trilho da Fóia	Monchique	Circular	7	360	Easy	2½	228
38	Pulo do Lobo	Guadiana Valley	Circular	5.5	250	Easy	3	231
39	GR23	Cachopo	Circular	46	1550	Challenging (2 days) or easy (4 days)	2–4 days	233
40	Serra do Caldeirão*	Parizes	Circular	20	840	Difficult	7	244

* walks can be split to create two shorter routes

APPENDIX B
Useful contacts

General information
The Instituto da Conservação da Natureza e da Florestas (ICNF) is responsible for all national and nature parks, and has much information including alternative walks in each park (www.icnf.pt). Visit Portugal is a good overview website, and has information about accommodation as well as walking companies (www.visitportugal.com).

Transport

Air

to Lisbon

Aerlingus
www.aerlingus.com

British Airways
www.britishairways.com

Easyjet
www.easyjet.com

Lufthansa
www.lufthansa.com

Ryanair
www.ryanair.com

TAP Portugal
www.flytap.com

to Porto

All the above except Aerlingus

to Faro

As per Lisbon plus:

Flybe
www.flybe.com

Jet2
www.jet2.com

Car
National road information
www.estradas.pt

Rail
Eurostar
www.eurostar.com

TGV train
www.sncf.com

Comboios de Portugal
www.cp.pt

Bus
Rede Expressos (consortium of bus companies)
www.rede-expressos.pt

Accommodation
Airbnb
www.airbnb.co.uk

TripAdvisor
www.tripadvisor.co.uk

Booking.com
www.booking.com

Maps
Instituto Geográphico do Exército (for the Carta Militar de Portugal)
www.igeoe.pt

Adventure Maps
www.adventuremaps.pt

Stanfords
www.stanfords.co.uk

m@pasonline
mapas.dgterritorio.pt

Opencycle
www.opencyclemap.org

Weather
Portuguese meteorological website
www.ipma.pt

meteoblue
www.meteoblue.com

Other walks
Tourist information offices are usually limited to a small selection of short local walks, with the notable exceptions being those at Manteigas (www.manteigastrilhosverdes. com), Monchique (www.cm-monchique.pt) and the park gates in Peneda-Gerês (adere-pg.pt). Maps and routes are highly variable in quality. Each town hall (*camara municipal*) is responsible for walks in its own area, and may have a website. For example, Idanha Nova provides information covering the Tejo area (www.cm-idanhanova. pt/turismo/percursos_pedestres.aspx – see 'Percursos Pedestres').

Walking Portugal (www.walkingportugal.com) has details of many more walks. Caminho Portuguesa is the Portuguese Camino de Santiago, and there are descriptions of the route, maps and places to stay at www.caminhoportuguesdesantiago.com. The schist villages have their own website with information, accommodation and more walks (www.aldeiasdoxisto.pt), as does Costa Vicentina (en.rotavicentina.com). For the Algarve, information on all of the Via Algarviana plus some other routes is available at www.viaalgarviana.org. A booklet containing 164 walks with other useful information can be downloaded from the Algarve website (www.visitalgarve.pt).

Emergencies
All emergencies (police, ambulance, fire service) tel 112
Forest fire tel 117
Poisons Information Centre for snake bites tel (+351) 808 250 143

APPENDIX C
Language

While Portuguese may share the Latin roots of the language in neighbouring Spain – hence the spelling looks so familiar – it most certainly does not sound similar. The Portuguese often say that they can understand the Spaniards very easily, yet the converse is not true. Especially in the north (see 'History'), you may find that French is widely spoken.

Useful phrases

English	Portuguese	pronunciation
Good morning	Bom dia	*Bong dee-a*
Good afternoon	Boa tarde	Boe tard
Hi	Olá	o-la
I'm sorry I don't speak Portuguese	Me desculpe, eu não falam Português	Mee shkulp, ee-you now falla Portu-gaysh
How are you?	Como está?	Com-eshta
Goodbye	Adeus	Adday-oosh
Do you speak English?	Fala inglês	Falla eeng-laysh
Where is the footpath to…?	Onde é a percurso pedestre para…?	Oon-day eh a per-curse-o ped-estree parra…?
Is it far?	É longe?	Eh lonj?
Can you repeat, please	Pode repetir, por favor	Pod rep-it-eer, poor fav-oor
Can you speak slowly	Pode falar devagar	Pod fallar vaggar
I don't understand	Não compreendo	Now com-preen-do
Excuse me	Faz favor	Fash fa-vor
Thank you	Obrigado (if you are a man)	Ob-ree-ga-doe
	Obrigada (if you are a woman)	Ob-ree-gaa-da
Yes/no	Sim/não	Sim/now

English	Portuguese	pronunciation
Left	À esquerda	Ah esh-kwerda
Right	À direita	Ah di-retta
Please	Por favor	Poor fav-oor
I'm OK/it is fine	Tudo bem	Too-doe beng
Straight ahead	Sempre em frente	Sem-pray em front-ay
There	Ali	Ah-lee
One	Um	Um
Two	Dois	Doy-sh
Three	Três	Tresh
Four	Quatro	Kwatro
Five	Cinco	Sinko
Six	Seis	Say-sh
Seven	Sete	Sett
Eight	Oito	Oyt-to
Nine	Nove	Nov
Ten	Dez	Desh

Glossary

Portuguese	English
albufeira	reservoir
barragem	dam
barranco	ravine
branda	summer grazing village, see Walk 3
cabo	cape
calçada	stone-built pavement, see Walk 11
caldas	hot springs
capela	chapel
casa	house
cascata	waterfall
castelo	castle

Portuguese	English
centro	centre (of town)
chã	level area
convento	convent
curral (plural currais)	corral, see Walk 10
ermida	hermitage
espigueiro	granary
fonte	fountain
herdade	homestead or manor house
inverneira	winter village
junta de freguesia	parish council building
largo	town/village square
lavadouro	communal clothes-washing place
levada	water channel
miradouro	viewpoint
moinho	mill (usually wind or water powered)
ponte	bridge
porta/portela	gate
pelourinho	pillory
pombal (plural pombais)	dovecote, see Walk 16
praia	beach
ribeira/ribeiro	stream (feminine/masculine)
rio	river
santuário	sanctuary
serra	mountain range
termas	spa
trilho	trail
velha/velho	old (feminine/masculine)
vila	village or town

DOWNLOAD THE ROUTES
IN GPX FORMAT

All the routes in this guide are available for download from:

www.cicerone.co.uk/889/GPX

as standard format GPX files. You should be able to load them into most online GPX systems and mobile devices, whether GPS or smartphone. You may need to convert the file into your preferred format using a conversion programme such as gpsvisualizer.com or one of the many other such websites and programmes.

When you follow this link, you will be asked for your email address and where you purchased the guidebook, and have the option to subscribe to the Cicerone e-newsletter.

www.cicerone.co.uk

LISTING OF CICERONE GUIDES

BRITISH ISLES CHALLENGES, COLLECTIONS AND ACTIVITIES

Cycling Land's End to John o' Groats
Great Walks on the England
  Coast Path
The Big Rounds
The Book of the Bivvy
The Book of the Bothy
The Mountains of England and
  Wales: Vol 1 Wales
The Mountains of England and
  Wales: Vol 2 England
The National Trails
Walking the End to End Trail

SHORT WALKS SERIES

Short Walks Hadrian's Wall
Short Walks in Arnside
  and Silverdale
Short Walks in Cornwall:
  Falmouth and the Lizard
Short Walks in Dumfries
  and Galloway
Short Walks in Nidderdale
Short Walks in Pembrokeshire:
  Tenby and the south
Short Walks in the South Downs:
  Brighton, Eastbourne and Arundel
Short Walks in the Surrey Hills
Short Walks Lake District – Coniston
  and Langdale
Short Walks Lake District: Keswick,
  Borrowdale and Buttermere
Short Walks Lake District:
  Windermere Ambleside and
  Grasmere
Short Walks on the Malvern Hills
Short Walks Winchester

SCOTLAND

Ben Nevis and Glen Coe
Cycling in the Hebrides
Cycling the North Coast 500
Great Mountain Days in Scotland
Mountain Biking in Southern and
  Central Scotland
Mountain Biking in West and North
  West Scotland
Not the West Highland Way
Scotland
Scotland's Best Small Mountains
Scotland's Mountain Ridges
Scottish Wild Country Backpacking
Skye's Cuillin Ridge Traverse
The Borders Abbeys Way
The Great Glen Way
The Great Glen Way Map Booklet
The Hebridean Way
The Hebrides
The Isle of Mull
The Isle of Skye
The Skye Trail

The Southern Upland Way
The West Highland Way
The West Highland Way
  Map Booklet
Walking Ben Lawers, Rannoch
  and Atholl
Walking in the Cairngorms
Walking in the Pentland Hills
Walking in the Scottish Borders
Walking in the Southern Uplands
Walking in Torridon, Fisherfield,
  Fannichs and An Teallach
Walking Loch Lomond and
  the Trossachs
Walking on Arran
Walking on Harris and Lewis
Walking on Jura, Islay and Colonsay
Walking on Rum and the Small Isles
Walking on the Orkney and
  Shetland Isles
Walking on Uist and Barra
Walking the Cape Wrath Trail
Walking the Corbetts
  Vol 1 South of the Great Glen
  Vol 2 North of the Great Glen
Walking the Galloway Hills
Walking the John o' Groats Trail
Walking the Munros
  Vol 1 – Southern, Central and
  Western Highlands
  Vol 2 – Northern Highlands and
  the Cairngorms
Winter Climbs in the Cairngorms
Winter Climbs: Ben Nevis and
  Glen Coe

NORTHERN ENGLAND ROUTES

Cycling the Reivers Route
Cycling the Way of the Roses
Hadrian's Cycleway
Hadrian's Wall Path
Hadrian's Wall Path Map Booklet
The Coast to Coast Cycle Route
The Coast to Coast Walk
The Coast to Coast Walk
  Map Booklet
The Pennine Way
The Pennine Way Map Booklet
Walking the Dales Way
Walking the Dales Way Map Booklet

NORTH-EAST ENGLAND, YORKSHIRE DALES AND PENNINES

Cycling in the Yorkshire Dales
Great Mountain Days in
  the Pennines
Mountain Biking in the
  Yorkshire Dales
The Cleveland Way and the
  Yorkshire Wolds Way
The North York Moors

Trail and Fell Running in the
  Yorkshire Dales
Walking in County Durham
Walking in Northumberland
Walking in the North Pennines
Walking in the Yorkshire Dales:
  North and East
  South and West
Walking St Cuthbert's Way
Walking St Oswald's Way and
  Northumberland Coast Path

NORTH-WEST ENGLAND AND THE ISLE OF MAN

Cycling the Pennine Bridleway
Isle of Man Coastal Path
The Lancashire Cycleway
The Lune Valley and Howgills
Walking in Cumbria's Eden Valley
Walking in Lancashire
Walking in the Forest of Bowland
  and Pendle
Walking on the Isle of Man
Walking on the West Pennine Moors
Walking the Ribble Way
Walks in Silverdale and Arnside

LAKE DISTRICT

Bikepacking in the Lake District
Cycling in the Lake District
Great Mountain Days in the
  Lake District
Joss Naylor's Lakes, Meres and
  Waters of the Lake District
Lake District Winter Climbs
Lake District:
  High Level and Fell Walks
  Low Level and Lake Walks
Mountain Biking in the Lake District
Outdoor Adventures with Children –
  Lake District
Scrambles in the Lake District –
  North
  South
Trail and Fell Running in the
  Lake District
Walking The Cumbria Way
Walking the Lake District Fells –
  Borrowdale
  Buttermere
  Coniston
  Keswick
  Langdale
  Mardale and the Far East
  Patterdale
  Wasdale
Walking the Tour of the Lake District

DERBYSHIRE, PEAK DISTRICT AND MIDLANDS

Cycling in the Peak District
Dark Peak Walks
Scrambles in the Dark Peak

Walking in Derbyshire
Walking in the Peak District –
   White Peak East
   White Peak West

SOUTHERN ENGLAND

20 Classic Sportive Rides in
   South East England
   South West England
Cycling in the Cotswolds
Mountain Biking on the
   North Downs
   South Downs
Suffolk Coast and Heath Walks
The Cotswold Way
The Cotswold Way Map Booklet
The Kennet and Avon Canal
The Lea Valley Walk
The North Downs Way
The North Downs Way Map Booklet
The Peddars Way and Norfolk
   Coast Path
The Pilgrims' Way
The Ridgeway National Trail
The Ridgeway National Trail
   Map Booklet
The South Downs Way
The South Downs Way Map Booklet
The Thames Path
The Thames Path Map Booklet
The Two Moors Way
The Two Moors Way Map Booklet
Walking Hampshire's Test Way
Walking in Cornwall
Walking in Essex
Walking in Kent
Walking in London
Walking in Norfolk
Walking in the Chilterns
Walking in the Cotswolds
Walking in the Isles of Scilly
Walking in the New Forest
Walking in the North Wessex Downs
Walking on Dartmoor
Walking on Guernsey
Walking on Jersey
Walking on the Isle of Wight
Walking the Dartmoor Way
Walking the Jurassic Coast
Walking the South West Coast Path
Walking the South West Coast Path
   Map Booklets
   – Vol 1: Minehead to St Ives
   – Vol 2: St Ives to Plymouth
   – Vol 3: Plymouth to Poole
Walks in the South Downs
   National Park

WALES AND WELSH BORDERS

Cycle Touring in Wales
Cycling Lon Las Cymru
Great Mountain Days in Snowdonia
Hillwalking in Shropshire
Mountain Walking in Snowdonia

Offa's Dyke Path
Offa's Dyke Path Map Booklet
Ridges of Snowdonia
Scrambles in Snowdonia
Snowdonia: 30 Low-level and
   Easy Walks
   – North
   – South
The Cambrian Way
The Pembrokeshire Coast Path
The Pembrokeshire Coast Path
   Map Booklet
The Snowdonia Way
Walking Glyndwr's Way
Walking in Carmarthenshire
Walking in Pembrokeshire
Walking in the Brecon Beacons
Walking in the Forest of Dean
Walking in the Wye Valley
Walking on Gower
Walking the Severn Way
Walking the Shropshire Way
Walking the Wales Coast Path

INTERNATIONAL CHALLENGES, COLLECTIONS AND ACTIVITIES

Europe's High Points
Walking the Via Francigena
   Pilgrim Route – Part 1

AFRICA

Kilimanjaro
Walking in the Drakensberg
Walks and Scrambles in the
   Moroccan Anti-Atlas

ALPS CROSS-BORDER ROUTES

100 Hut Walks in the Alps
Alpine Ski Mountaineering
   Vol 1 – Western Alps
The Karnischer Hohenweg
The Tour of the Bernina
Trail Running – Chamonix and the
   Mont Blanc region
Trekking Chamonix to Zermatt
Trekking in the Alps
Trekking in the Silvretta and
   Ratikon Alps
Trekking Munich to Venice
Trekking the Tour du Mont Blanc
Trekking the Tour du Mont Blanc
   Map Booklet
Walking in the Alps

PYRENEES AND FRANCE/SPAIN CROSS-BORDER ROUTES

Shorter Treks in the Pyrenees
The Pyrenean Haute Route
The Pyrenees
Trekking the GR11 Trail
Walks and Climbs in the Pyrenees

AUSTRIA

Innsbruck Mountain Adventures
Trekking Austria's Adlerweg
Trekking in Austria's Hohe Tauern
Trekking in Austria's Zillertal Alps
Trekking in the Stubai Alps
Walking in Austria
Walking in the Salzkammergut:
   the Austrian Lake District

EASTERN EUROPE

The Danube Cycleway Vol 2
The High Tatras
The Mountains of Romania
Walking in Hungary

FRANCE, BELGIUM AND LUXEMBOURG

Camino de Santiago – Via Podiensis
Chamonix Mountain Adventures
Cycle Touring in France
Cycling London to Paris
Cycling the Canal de la Garonne
Cycling the Canal du Midi
Cycling the Route des Grandes Alpes
Mont Blanc Walks
Mountain Adventures in
   the Maurienne
Short Treks on Corsica
The Elbe Cycle Route
The GR5 Trail
The GR5 Trail – Benelux and
   Lorraine
The GR5 Trail – Vosges and Jura
The Grand Traverse of the
   Massif Central
The Moselle Cycle Route
The River Loire Cycle Route
The River Rhone Cycle Route
Trekking in the Vanoise
Trekking the Cathar Way
Trekking the GR10
Trekking the GR20 Corsica
Trekking the Robert Louis
   Stevenson Trail
Via Ferratas of the French Alps
Walking in Provence – East
Walking in Provence – West
Walking in the Ardennes
Walking in the Auvergne
Walking in the Brianconnais
Walking in the Dordogne
Walking in the Haute Savoie: North
Walking in the Haute Savoie: South
Walking on Corsica
Walking the Brittany Coast Path

GERMANY

Hiking and Cycling in the
   Black Forest
The Danube Cycleway Vol 1
The Rhine Cycle Route
The Westweg
Walking in the Bavarian Alps

IRELAND

The Wild Atlantic Way and Western Ireland
Walking the Wicklow Way

ITALY

Alta Via – Trekking in the Dolomites – Vols 1&2
Day Walks in the Dolomites
Italy's Grande Traversata delle Alpi
Italy's Sibillini National Park
Ski Touring and Snowshoeing in the Dolomites
The Way of St Francis
Trekking in the Apennines
Trekking the Giants' Trail: Alta Via 1 through the Italian Pennine Alps
Via Ferratas of the Italian Dolomites – Vols 1&2
Walking in Abruzzo
Walking in Italy's Cinque Terre
Walking in Italy's Stelvio National Park
Walking in Sicily
Walking in the Aosta Valley
Walking in the Dolomites
Walking in Tuscany
Walking in Umbria
Walking Lake Como and Maggiore
Walking Lake Garda and Iseo
Walking on the Amalfi Coast
Walking the Via Francigena Pilgrim Route – Parts 2&3
Walks and Treks in the Maritime Alps

MEDITERRANEAN

The High Mountains of Crete
Trekking in Greece
Walking and Trekking in Zagori
Walking and Trekking on Corfu
Walking in Cyprus
Walking on Malta
Walking on the Greek Islands – the Cyclades

NEW ZEALAND AND AUSTRALIA

Hiking the Overland Track

NORTH AMERICA

Hiking and Cycling the California Missions Trail
The John Muir Trail
The Pacific Crest Trail

SOUTH AMERICA

Aconcagua and the Southern Andes
Hiking and Biking Peru's Inca Trails
Trekking in Torres del Paine

SCANDINAVIA, ICELAND AND GREENLAND

Hiking in Norway – South
Trekking in Greenland – The Arctic Circle Trail
Trekking the Kungsleden
Walking and Trekking in Iceland

SLOVENIA, CROATIA, SERBIA, MONTENEGRO AND ALBANIA

Hiking Slovenia's Juliana Trail
Mountain Biking in Slovenia
The Islands of Croatia
The Julian Alps of Slovenia
The Mountains of Montenegro
The Peaks of the Balkans Trail
The Slovene Mountain Trail
Walking in Slovenia: The Karavanke
Walks and Treks in Croatia

SPAIN AND PORTUGAL

Camino de Santiago: Camino Frances
Coastal Walks in Andalucia
Costa Blanca Mountain Adventures
Cycling the Camino de Santiago
Cycling the Ruta Via de la Plata
Mountain Walking in Mallorca
Mountain Walking in Southern Catalunya
Portugal's Rota Vicentina
Spain's Sendero Historico: The GR1
The Andalucian Coast to Coast Walk
The Camino del Norte and Camino Primitivo
The Camino Ingles and Ruta do Mar
The Camino Portugues
The Mountains Around Nerja
The Mountains of Ronda and Grazalema
The Sierras of Extremadura
Trekking in Mallorca
Trekking in the Canary Islands
Trekking the GR7 in Andalucia
Walking and Trekking in the Sierra Nevada
Walking in Andalucia
Walking in Catalunya – Barcelona
Walking in Catalunya – Girona Pyrenees
Walking in Portugal
Walking in the Algarve
Walking in the Picos de Europa
Walking La Via de la Plata and Camino Sanabres
Walking on Gran Canaria
Walking on La Gomera and El Hierro
Walking on La Palma
Walking on Lanzarote and Fuerteventura

Walking on Madeira
Walking on Tenerife
Walking on the Azores
Walking on the Costa Blanca
Walking the Camino dos Faros

SWITZERLAND

Switzerland's Jura Crest Trail
The Swiss Alps
Tour of the Jungfrau Region
Trekking the Swiss Via Alpina
Walking in the Bernese Oberland – Jungfrau region
Walking in the Engadine – Switzerland
Walking in the Valais
Walking in Ticino
Walking in Zermatt and Saas-Fee

CHINA, JAPAN AND ASIA

Hiking and Trekking in the Japan Alps and Mount Fuji
Hiking in Hong Kong
Japan's Kumano Kodo Pilgrimage
Trekking in Tajikistan

HIMALAYA

Annapurna
8000 metres
Everest: A Trekker's Guide
Trekking in Bhutan
Trekking in Ladakh
Trekking in the Himalaya
Trekking in the Karakoram

MOUNTAIN LITERATURE

A Walk in the Clouds
Abode of the Gods
Fifty Years of Adventure
The Pennine Way – the Path, the People, the Journey
Unjustifiable Risk?
Unjustifiable Risk?

TECHNIQUES

Fastpacking
Geocaching in the UK
Map and Compass
Outdoor Photography
The Mountain Hut Book

MINI GUIDES

Alpine Flowers
Navigation
Pocket First Aid and Wilderness Medicine
Snow

For full information on all our guides, books and eBooks, visit our website:
www.cicerone.co.uk

CICERONE

Trust Cicerone to guide your next adventure,
wherever it may be around the world...

Discover guides for hiking, mountain walking, backpacking,
trekking, trail running, cycling and mountain biking, ski touring,
climbing and scrambling in Britain, Europe and worldwide.

Connect with Cicerone online and find inspiration.

- buy books and ebooks
- articles, advice and trip reports
- podcasts and live events
- GPX files and updates
- regular newsletter

cicerone.co.uk